Name ______________________________ ____

Write the numeral in the box that expla

MW01437729

Who Said

1. Happy Birthday!
2. I'm high in the sky.
3. I'm so sleepy.
4. This tastes so good.
5. I love to read.
6. We won!
7. I like the rain.
8. Did you brush your teeth?

© Frank Schaffer Publications, Inc.

Name ______________________________

Write the numeral under the picture that goes with the sentence.

What Tool Would You Use?

1. Please cut the bread, John.
2. A nail goes here, Sally.
3. This ice cream tastes yummy.
4. Cut this wood in half, please.
5. Can you hold the bolt tighter.?
6. This will help you push the needle, Sue.
7. Cut the paper in half.
8. Mom, the eye is too small.

© Frank Schaffer Publications, Inc.

Name ____

Write the numeral in the box that explains the sentence.

All About Christmas!

1. He had a very shiny nose.
2. He brings presents.
3. The Christmas balls keep falling off.
4. No two are ever alike.
5. We need coal, a carrot, and a hat.
6. Hang it on the chimney.

© Frank Schaffer Publications, Inc.

Name ______________________________

Write the numeral in the box that explains the sentence.

What's the Weather?

1. Now we can ski.
2. Teddy needed an umbrella today.
3. It was hard to see across the street.
4. My kite flew as high as I could see.
5. We are ready for the beach.
6. I think it will rain today.

snow ☐

sunny ☐

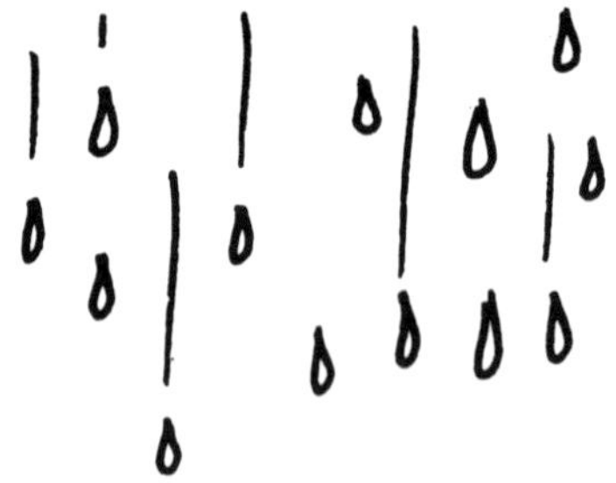

rain ☐

cloudy ☐

windy ☐

foggy ☐

© Frank Schaffer Publications, Inc.

Name ______________________________

Write the numeral in the box that tells how you can tell . . . .

Use Your Senses

1. The girl is singing.
2. The skunk is angry.
3. The food is good.
4. The trees are green.
5. The stove is hot.

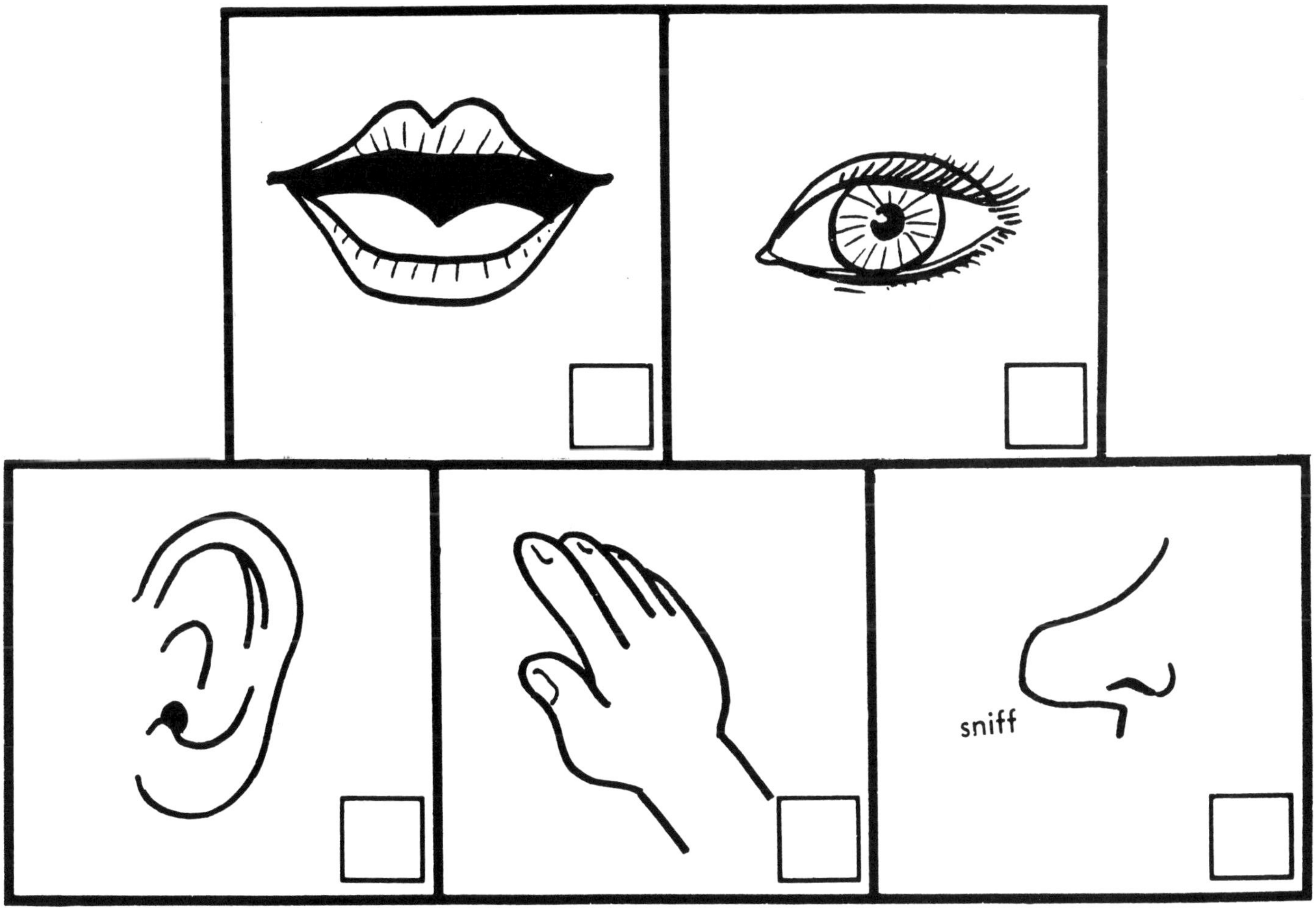

© Frank Schaffer Publications, Inc.

Name ____________________

Write the numeral in the box that goes with the sentence.

How Would You Feel?

1. You ran as fast as you could to school.
2. You went to bed too late.
3. Your best friend got the measles.
4. You got a new bike for your birthday.
5. The pieces didn't fit.
6. Your sister poked you.

mad ☐

sad ☐

hot and tired ☐

puzzled ☐

sleepy ☐

happy ☐

© Frank Schaffer Publications, Inc.

Name ____________________

Write the numeral in the box that explains the sentence.

Where Will It Happen?

1. Jeff is going to go on a trip in the air.
2. Tom had his tonsils out.
3. My family is visiting the animals.
4. I have fun riding with my friends.
5. Janet is watching T.V.
6. We saw the clowns and tight-rope walkers.
7. Let's build a sand castle.
8. I'm getting a cool glass of milk.

© Frank Schaffer Publications, Inc.

Name ____________________

Write the numeral under the picture that explains the sentence.

How Would You Get There?

1. The children are ready to go to school.
2. My mother drove to work.
3. It's a long trip across the ocean.
4. My friend and I pedaled to the library.
5. We went straight up!
6. Dad paid the man for the ride.
7. We zoomed down the track.
8. We flew right over the clouds.

© Frank Schaffer Publications, Inc.

Name ____________________

Write the numeral under the picture that explains the sentence.

Where Do They Live?

1. The bear slept all through the winter.
2. The puppy curled up and went to sleep.
3. The boy had some toys in his room.
4. She kept her eggs warm.
5. They swim in a school.
6. The hamster hid in the straw.
7. The chief wore green feathers.
8. Six dogs pulled their sled.

cave	nest	cage	doghouse

igloo	**house**	**ocean**	**tepee**

Name ____________________

What Do You Need . . .?

1. to write a newspaper story?
2. to take a picture of a baby?
3. to play in a band?
4. to be a pilot?
5. to be a baseball player?
6. to build a house?
7. to paint a picture?
8. to make clothes?
9. to fix the sink?
10. to sweep the floor?

Name____

Write the numeral in the box that explains the sentence.

Who Said It?

1. The boys and girls left the room messy.
2. Someone dropped a spoon down the sink.
3. The food is sticking to the bottom of the pan.
4. The grass grew high after the rain.
5. That will be $5.82, please.
6. I'm going to listen to your heart beat.
7. I have very long hoses on my truck.
8. Please be very quiet.

© Frank Schaffer Publications, Inc.

Name ____________________

Write the numeral under the picture that explains the sentence.

What Holiday Is It?

1. Santa Claus is coming to town.
2. John sent candy to his girlfriend.
3. Did you make a wish?
4. Today we give thanks.
5. That is a very scary mask.
6. How many eggs did you find?
7. The fireworks are beautiful.
8. Are you wearing green today?

© Frank Schaffer Publications, Inc.

Name ______________________________

Write the numeral in the box that explains the sentence.

Buzz — Bite — Bark — Meow!

1. Buzz - - - - - - - - - - - sting!
2. Ruff, ruff ruff!
3. Meow, meow — Meowwwwwwwwwww!
4. Gobble, gobble, gobble.
5. Peep, peep, peep.
6. Baa, Baa, Baa, Baa !
7. Oink, oink, oink.
8. Neigh, neigh, neigh, neigh!

© Frank Schaffer Publications, Inc.

Name ____

Write the numeral under the picture that goes with the sentence.

What's the Sport?

1. Come on team, make a touchdown.
2. Hit the ball out of the park!
3. They were trying to hit the puck.
4. Dribble the ball down the court.
5. You can hit the ball with your head!
6. Grandad got a hole-in-one.
7. Your serve!
8. Aim for the head pin, Mark.

© Frank Schaffer Publications, Inc.

Name ____________________

Write the numeral under the picture that goes with the sentence.

What Would You Wear?

1. The waves are not very big.
2. Eric had crooked teeth.
3. Mother told me I could step in the puddles.
4. Don't crash!
5. I'm baking fudge brownies!
6. Don't freeze your fingers!
7. It was hard for me to see the blackboard.
8. Don't forget to wind it!

© Frank Schaffer Publications, Inc.

Name ____________________

Write the numeral under the picture that goes with the sentence.

What is the Food?

1. Pour me a tall glass, please.
2. Say, it slips off my fork!
3. All I need is jelly to make me happy.
4. We had a good Thanksgiving dinner.
5. I like this sandwich!
6. Fry it nice and crisp.
7. The rabbits ate all day long.
8. My teeth felt very cold.

Name ______________________________

Write the numeral under the picture that goes with the sentence.

What Happened Before?

1. Mother answered the telephone.
2. It started to rain.
3. The flower grew.
4. Fred fell down. Ouch!
5. The boy went to bed.
6. The alarm clock went "buzz"!
7. We ate dinner.
8. The baseball went over the fence.

© Frank Schaffer Publications, Inc.

Name ______________________________

Write the numeral in the box that explains the sentence.

What Am I?

1. I am small, and I make honey.
2. I am large, and I swim in water.
3. I can fly and have webbed feet.
4. I go "cluck, cluck," and I give you eggs.
5. I have stripes and live in Africa.
6. I am furry and come from Australia.

Name ____

Write the numeral in the box that tells about the thing that moves.

Moving Things

1. These go on the feet and have blades.
2. This is side-walk surfing with wheels.
3. I can ride the waves with this.
4. This has two wheels and a motor.
5. This has a powerful engine and goes into space.
6. This goes on tracks and pulls many cars.

© Frank Schaffer Publications, Inc.

Name ____

Write the numeral under the picture that explains the sentence.

What Time of Day is it?

1. I hear the lunch bell.
2. It's almost the next day.
3. Now I can see the stars.
4. The sun just went down.
5. Yum, we're having pancakes for breakfast.
6. The sun is coming up behind the hills.

Name ____________________

My Favorite Books

Lila loves to read. These are the books she likes best.

fold -- fold

Put an X on Lila's favorite books.

Number right ____________

Number wrong ____________

Brainwork! What are the names of your favorite books?

Name ____________________

Mrs. Clark's Class

fold -- fold

Put a box around everything that you saw in the classroom above.

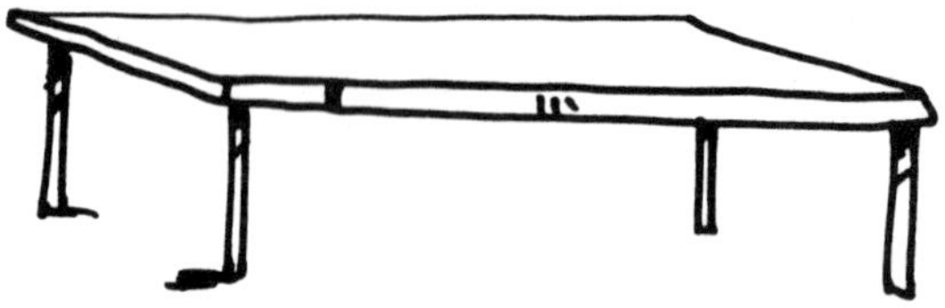

Number right ____________

Number wrong ____________

Brainwork! Which of the things on this page are in your classroom?

© Frank Schaffer Publications, Inc.

Name ______________________________

Foot Traffic

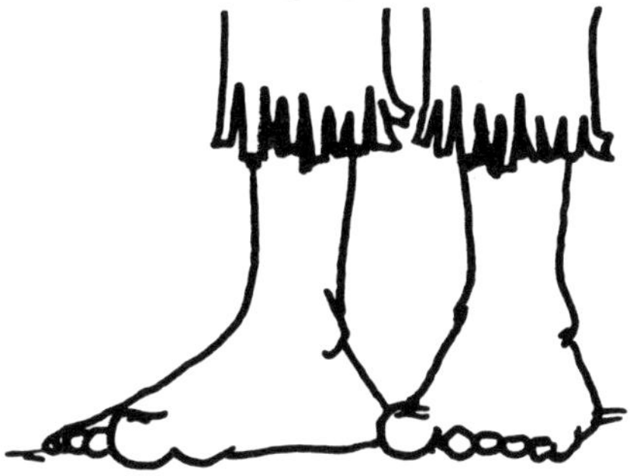

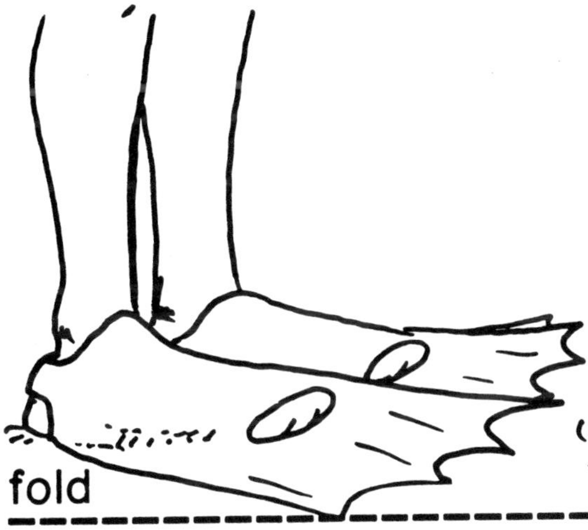

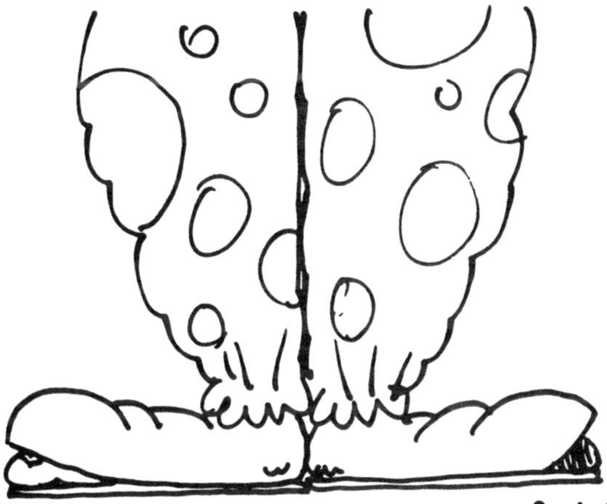

fold   fold

Color the feet that are just like the ones above.

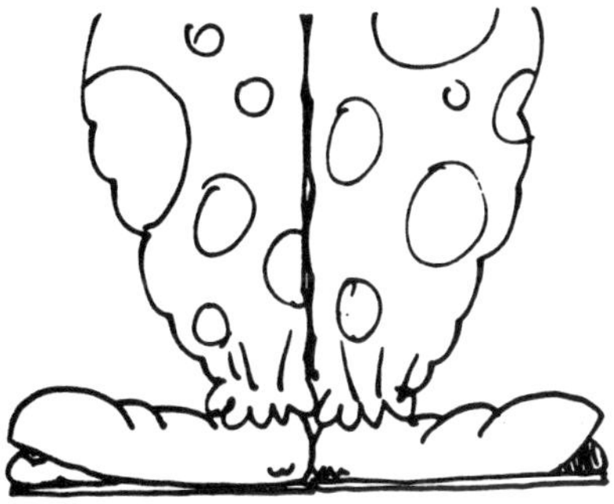
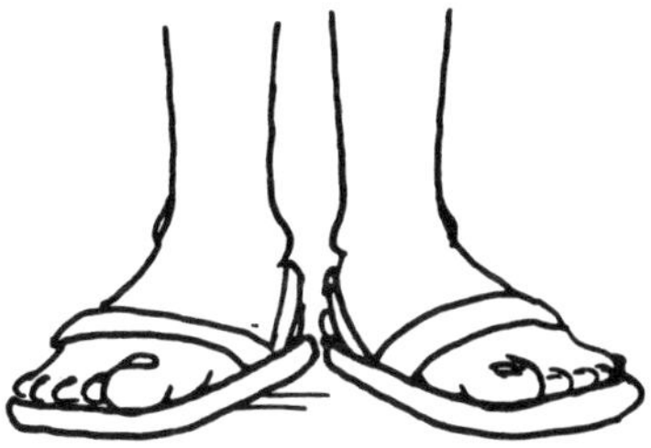
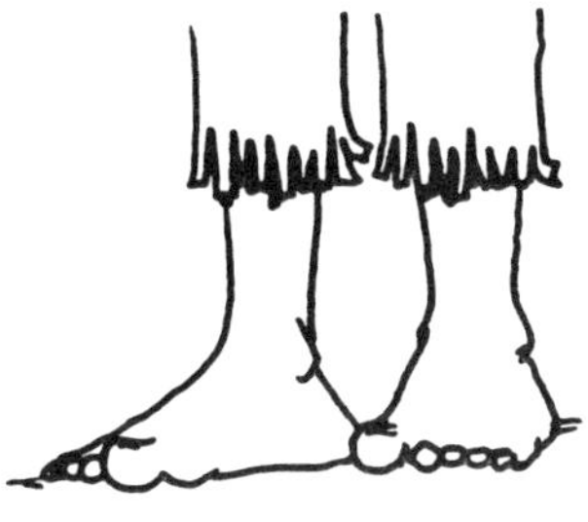

Number right ______________

Number wrong ______________

Brainwork! Draw your own feet!

© Frank Schaffer Publications, Inc.

Name ____

Pete's Picnic

fold fold

How many of each of these were at Pete's picnic?

 __________

 __________

 __________

 __________

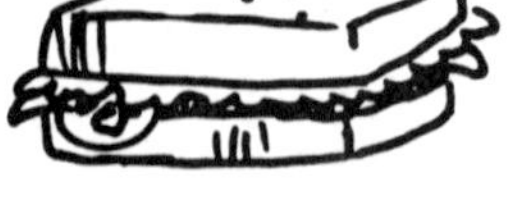 __________

 __________

Number right ______________

Number wrong ______________

Brainwork! What are four of your favorite picnic foods?

Name

Animal Word Shapes

In the story below, the names of animals are missing. Use the shape of the missing word to help you find the name in the Word Box. Write the words inside the shapes. Example: The [monkey] had a long tail.

Our class went to the zoo. We saw a tall [giraffe] munching on leaves. The [ ] were taking a bath. Perched in a tree was a sleeping [ ]. A [ ] roared in its den. A [ ] hopped close behind its mother. The [ ] scurried up the side of a tree. Three [ ] were coiled on a rock. Playful [ ] barked and dove for fish. The [ ] searched for peanuts with its trunk. Six [ ] floated on the pond. The big [ ] beat its chest. Many [ ] hung upside down in a dark room. As we walked by, a [ ] said, "Hello." It was fun to see so many animals, but my favorite was the [ ] with the big antlers.

Word Box

squirrel
snakes
hippos
kangaroo
elephant
gorilla
lion
moose
giraffe
seals
ducks
eagle
bats
parrot

Try This! Neatly write the names of five animals in dark crayon. Leave space between them. Lay a fresh paper on top. Trace the shapes of the words. Cut the shapes out and scramble the pieces. Write each animal's name in its shape.

© Frank Schaffer Publications, Inc.

Name

Animals and Their Babies

The names of eight animals and their babies are hidden in this puzzle. First fill in the name of the missing animals or babies. Then circle each of the words in the puzzle. The animals are written across →, down ↓, and diagonally ↘.

k________	joey	bear	c________
cat	k________	d________	duckling
sheep	l________	dog	p________
h________	foal	c________	calf

Word Box

- bear
- calf
- cat
- cow
- cub
- dog
- duck
- duckling
- foal
- horse
- joey
- kangaroo
- kitten
- lamb
- puppy
- sheep

k	i	t	t	e	n	w	o	r	k
a	n	d	u	c	k	l	i	n	g
n	h	e	u	n	f	e	a	a	r
g	o	t	e	c	o	w	o	m	e
a	r	t	i	s	k	a	b	e	b
r	s	h	e	e	p	b	e	a	r
o	e	q	u	i	e	u	t	r	j
o	c	a	t	d	i	g	p	t	o
m	u	l	f	o	a	l	d	p	e
s	b	a	n	g	c	a	l	f	y

Try This! List eight more animals you know. Hide them in a word search puzzle. Switch with a friend and work each other's puzzle.

© Frank Schaffer Publications, Inc.

Name______________________________ Skill: Classification

Go-Togethers

Look at each group of words below. First cross out the word that does not belong. Then add a word from the Word Box that does belong.

Word Box

refrigerator **sweater** **fountain** **towel** **scissors** **shovel**

1.

paper
eraser
penguin
pencil
stapler
glue

2.

toothbrush
mirror
soap
sausage
sink
washcloth

3.

pans
dishes
globe
stove
cupboard
toaster

4.

shirts
skirts
pants
soil
shoes
socks

5.

chocolate
lawnmower
paint
hose
tools
clippers

6.

swings
pond
grass
benches
flowers
pound

Brainwork! For each list above complete this title: "Things You'd Find In..."

© Frank Schaffer Publications, Inc.

Name ____________________ Skill: Context clues

What Does It Mean?

Choose a word from the Word Box to replace the boldfaced word in each sentence. Write it on the line. A dictionary can help you.

Word Box				
shake	brave	smell	copy	little
strong	tease	choose	disappear	

1. The mouse felt **puny** standing next to the elephant.

2. Sour milk can have a bad **odor.**

3. I get mad when big kids **taunt** my sister.

4. The people will **elect** a new president.

5. It was so cold I began to **quiver.**

6. These trees look **sturdy** enough to climb.

7. I saw the light in the distance **vanish.**

8. My brother can **imitate** the sound of a bird.

9. The **courageous** knight fought the mean dragon.

Brainwork! Choose two of the sentences above to illustrate.

© Frank Schaffer Publications, Inc.

Name ________________ Skill: Context clues

In Other Words

Choose a word from the Word Box to replace the boldfaced word in each sentence.

Let's exchange places.

Yes, let's trade places.

Word Box

trade	smile	hit	shine	path
spin	move	burn	extra	dressed

1. She can really **whack** the ball. ________________
2. The dancer began to **twirl.** ________________
3. I couldn't **budge** the heavy box. ________________
4. The teacher said to **exchange** papers. ________________
5. The silly joke made him **grin.** ________________
6. A hot iron can **scorch** clothes. ________________
7. The **spare** tire is in the trunk. ________________
8. We followed the **trail** back to camp. ________________
9. Waxing the car made it **gleam.** ________________
10. The king was **clad** in royal robes. ________________

Brainwork! Write three sentences that might make a friend grin. Exchange papers and find out if they do!

© Frank Schaffer Publications, Inc.

Name ______________________ Skill: Context clues

Learning to Skate

Read this story about learning to skate. Then answer the questions.

Many times I had **longed** to be able to ice skate. Finally my big sister agreed to teach me.

I was filled with **glee** as I laced up my skates for the first time. I thought I would be **gliding** over the ice in minutes. Was I surprised when I stood up and fell right on the ice. It sure was **chilly**!

My sister helped me up and said, "Don't **fret**. After a few more **tumbles** you'll be skating like a star!"

1. Which boldfaced word in the story means:

a. cold? ______________ d. worry? ______________

b. wished? ______________ e. moving? ______________

c. joy? ______________ f. falls? ______________

2. Circle the best answer.

a. The word **chilly** has to do with

food temperature skates

b. Which would most likely fill you with **glee**?

being sick a surprise party

c. Which would you most likely **long** for?

a missing toy a broken pencil

d. When would you be most likely to **fret**?

if you missed the school bus if you got a good grade

Brainwork! Draw and label five things that can glide through the air or on the water.

© Frank Schaffer Publications, Inc.

What's the Question?

In each conversation below, the answer to a question is given but the question is missing! Choose and write the question from the Question Box that asks for the answer given. A sample is done for you.

What day is it?

It's Tuesday.

Question Box

What time is it?	How old are you?	How's the weather?
How much did it cost?	How are you?	What's for lunch?

1.  ______________________ It was $1.95. 

2.  ______________________ It's warm and sunny. 

3.  ______________________ It's 11:30 A.M. 

4.  ______________________ We're having hot dogs. 

5.  ______________________ I'm eight years old. 

6.  ______________________ I'm fine, thank you. 

Try This! Write the answers to three easy questions. Have a friend guess the questions.

© Frank Schaffer Publications, Inc.

Name ______________________ Skill: Multiple meanings

Different Meanings

Look at the list below. Two different meanings are given for each word.

sign	1) a symbol	2) to write your name
dash	1) a small amount	2) to run quickly
chief	1) leader	2) first or main
trip	1) journey	2) to stumble
quarter	1) one-fourth	2) 25¢ coin
company	1) visitor or guests	2) business

Decide which meaning the boldfaced word has in each sentence below. Fill in (1) or (2). Then write the meaning on the line.

(1) (2) A. Be careful not to **trip** over the rock!

(1) (2) B. We are having **company** tonight.

(1) (2) C. When it started to rain we made a **dash** for the house.

(1) (2) D. They turned left at the stop **sign.**

(1) (2) E. Mom gave me a **quarter** for my piggy bank.

(1) (2) F. The **chief** of police spoke to us about safety.

Brainwork! Write a new sentence for every boldfaced word. Have each sentence show the word's other meaning.

© Frank Schaffer Publications, Inc.

Name ______________________________ Skill: Multiple meanings

Which Scale?

Read these different meanings for the word **scale**.

1) thin plates on reptiles or fish.
2) an object used to measure weight
3) to climb up the side
4) a map marking for distance
5) a group of musical notes

1. Which meaning of **scale** (1, 2, 3, 4, or 5) does each picture show?

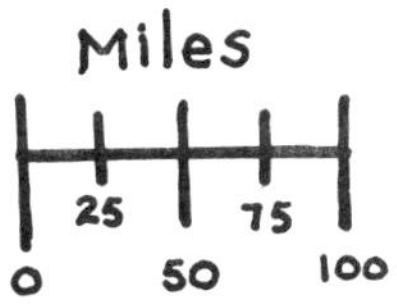

2. Choose the correct meaning of **scale** in each sentence. Write the meaning on the line below the sentence.

A. The **scale** shows that the town is 15 miles away.

B. Many dinosaurs had **scales**.

C. I can play **scales** on the piano.

D. She put the meat on a **scale**.

E. He **scaled** the high mountain.

Brainwork! Look up the word **mark** in a dictionary. Write five of its meanings.

© Frank Schaffer Publications, Inc.

Name

State Puzzle Poems

Do you know these states? Read the clues below. Write the name of the state on the line below its poem. Then write the state's two-letter abbreviation on its shape.

Florida (FL)
Alaska (AK)
Pennsylvania (PA)
California (CA)
Texas (TX)
Tennessee (TN)

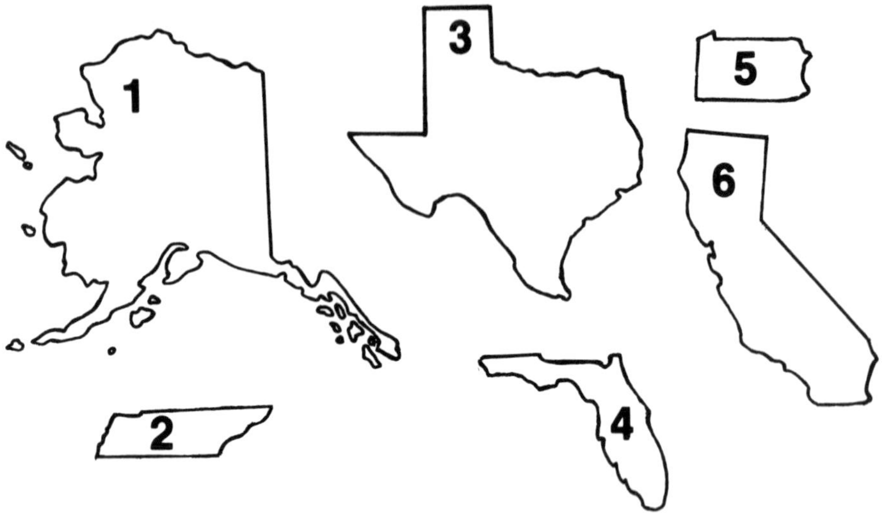

1. It's the largest state
   and gets lots of snow.
   You'll need a parka
   to go there, you know.

   ____

2. Nashville's the capital of
   the Volunteer State.
   And at its Ol' Opry
   the music's just great!

   ____

3. Everything's big here
   that we all know,
   With Houston, Dallas,
   and the famed Alamo.

   ____

4. Palm trees and oranges
   and bright sunny beaches,
   To the southernmost point
   in the U.S. it reaches.

   ____

5. Named for William Penn
   or so I've heard tell,
   And here you can find
   the Liberty Bell.

   ____

6. The Golden Gate bridge
   and the tall redwood trees
   Are two of its places
   most likely to please.

   ____

Try This! Make up your own poem about another state. Trace its shape from a map. Then trade your state puzzle with a friend.

© Frank Schaffer Publications, Inc.

Name ______________________ Skill: Social studies vocabulary, Context

Needs and Wants

Read this story about working together. The boldfaced words may be new to you. Their meanings are given below the story. Write the word that matches each meaning.

People everywhere have the same needs. They all need food, clothing, and shelter to **survive**, or stay alive.

In a community people **cooperate**, or work together, to get the things they need.

Some people provide **goods**, which are things made or grown for people to use. Other people provide **services**, or jobs that help others.

Besides needs, there are many things people want to make their lives more comfortable or fun. They buy many goods and services to enjoy in their **leisure**, or free time.

1. ______________ work together
2. ______________ free time
3. ______________ stay alive
4. ______________ things made or grown for people to use
5. ______________ jobs people do for each other

The pictures show jobs people do. Label them **goods** or **services**.

A.  ______________

B.  ______________

Brainwork! Draw and label ten pictures of goods and services you use.

© Frank Schaffer Publications, Inc.

Name ______________________ Skill: Science vocabulary, Context

Looking for Energy

Read this story about energy. The boldfaced words may be new to you. Their meanings are given below the story. Write the word that matches each meaning.

Scientists are looking for new **sources**, or places, to get energy. They are finding new ways to make, or **produce**, the power we will need in the future.

One kind of energy is **geothermal**. "Geo" means "earth" and "thermal" means "heat." Geothermal energy comes from heat that is already stored inside the earth.

Another kind of energy is **solar**. "Sol" means "sun." The sunlight is changed into energy we can use.

1. ______________ heat from the earth
2. ______________ from the sun
3. ______________ to make
4. ______________ places to get something

These pictures show kinds of energy. Label them **geothermal** or **solar**.

A.

____

B.

____

Brainwork! "-ology" means "the study of." Write what you think **geology** means. Then write the dictionary definition.

Name

That's Nonsense!

In each sentence below, the boldfaced word is not a real word. Even though the word is nonsense, you will be able to tell what it means from the way it's used. Choose a word from the Word Box to replace the nonsense word in each sentence.

a what?

Write the new sentences.

1. I had a **dringel** for lunch.

   ____

2. I read three **bleeks** last week.

   ____

3. The **rawgis** took my temperature.

   ____

4. I wrote my name with a **jilcin**.

   ____

5. I'm **thaker** than my little brother.

   ____

6. I enjoy **strobbing** in the pool.

   ____

7. I brush my **seetles** every day.

   ____

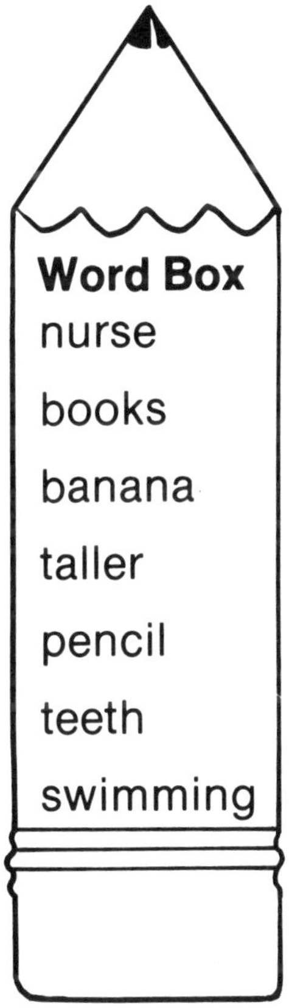
Word Box
nurse
books
banana
taller
pencil
teeth
swimming

Draw a "dringel."	Draw a "rawgis."	Draw a "jilcin."

Try This! Invent your own nonsense words for: *school, bus, teacher, homework,* and *classroom.* Write a story that uses all of your invented words. Read it to a friend. Have him guess what your words stand for.

© Frank Schaffer Publications, Inc.

Name

Sign Language

People who cannot hear or speak are able to "talk" with their hands by using sign language. Many words and phrases have their own sign. All words can also be signed by finger-spelling using the **manual alphabet.**

Manual Alphabet

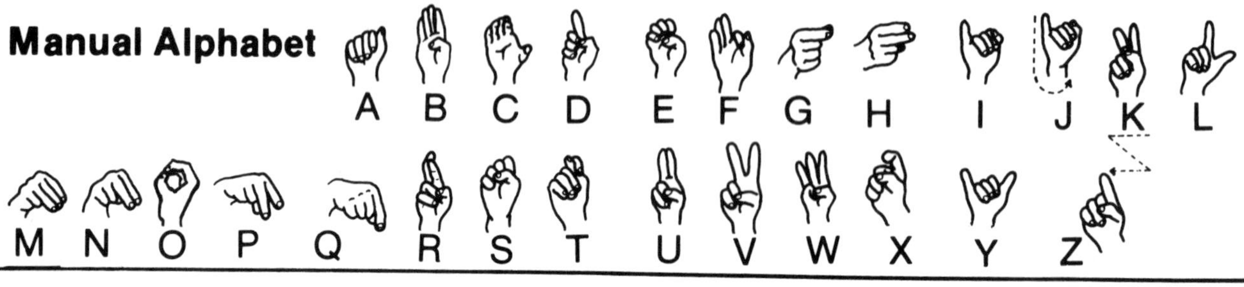
A B C D E F G H I J K L
M N O P Q R S T U V W X Y Z

Can you read these words? Write the letter below each sign.

___ ___ ___ ___ ___ ___ ___   ___ ___   ___ ___ ___

Practice signing the alphabet. Then sign the words and phrases below.

book

school
(clap twice)

Please

Thank you

My

name (is)
(tap twice)

T a s h a

Try This! Tasha has signed her name for a friend. Try spelling your name using sign language.

© Frank Schaffer Publications, Inc.

Crack the Code

Use the code to write the correct letter below each symbol. You will discover the answers to some riddles. Draw a picture of each answer as you solve the riddle.  (BEGIN).

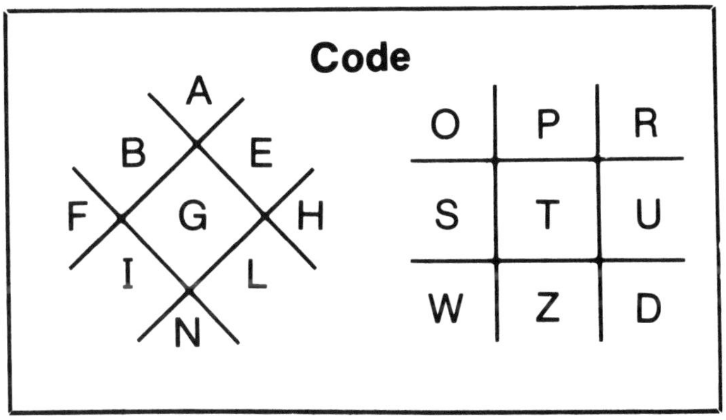

Example:
What do you always look toward but never see?

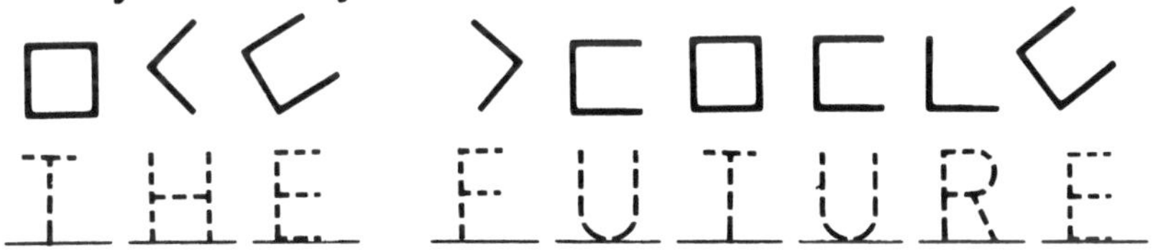

1. What gets wetter the more it dries?  _ _ _ _ _	2. What falls but never breaks?  _ _ _ _
3. What has eyes but no face?  _ _ _ _ _ _ _	4. What grows without getting any bigger?  _ _ _ _ _ _ _ _ _ _ _ _ _

Try This! Think of one of your favorite riddles. Write it and put the answer in code for a friend to solve.

© Frank Schaffer Publications, Inc.

Rebus Fun

Letters, numbers, and pictures take the place of words in each sentence below. Use the Code Box to help you decode the sentences. Then write each sentence in your best handwriting.

Code Box

R	are		leaves	e	handy		I
8	ate		can	m	my	BBB	bees
L	elbow		notebook	2	two	c	fancy
p	keep	B4	before	t	belt	r	skater
u	you						

1. He  B4 u .

2. u have a c t .

3. 2 BBB stung m L .

4. p your  e .

5.  8 a  of soup.

6. R u a good r ?

Try This! Write a message to a friend using some rebus words from the Code Box. Exchange papers to decode each other's message.

© Frank Schaffer Publications, Inc.

Name ______________________ Skill: Decoding

Word Detective

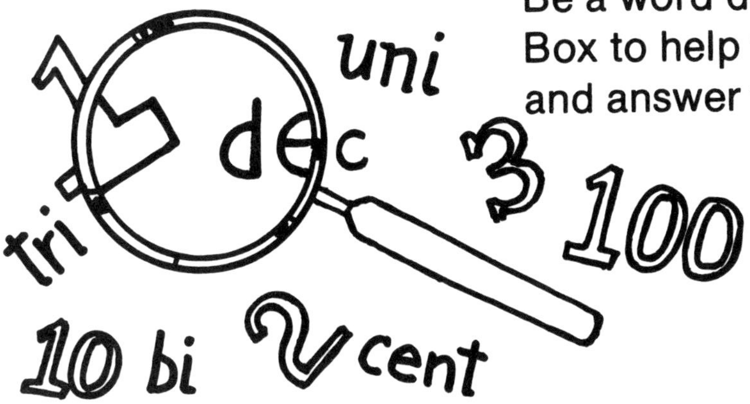

Be a word detective. Use the clues in the Clue Box to help you decode the boldfaced words and answer the questions.

Clue Box

uni- one	**tri-** three
bi- two	**dec-** ten
cent- one hundred	

1. How many years in a **century**? ____________
2. How many wheels on a **bicycle**? ____________
3. How many angles in a **triangle**? ____________
4. How many years in a **decade**? ____________
5. How many legs on a **centipede**? ____________
6. How many horns on a **unicorn**? ____________
7. How many years in a **centennial**? ____________
8. How many wheels on a **unicycle**? ____________
9. How many legs on a **decapod**? ____________
10. How many horns on a **triceratops**? ____________

Brainwork! Draw and label a unicycle, a bicycle, a tricycle. Write which you think would be the hardest to ride and why.

© Frank Schaffer Publications, Inc.

Name

Compound Confusion

The sentences below sound silly because one of the words that form the compound is incorrect. Choose a word from the Word Box to take the place of the boldfaced part of the word. Write the sentence correctly.

Word Box

drops rise run chalk works
prints water shake suit

Example: The teacher wrote on the **checker**board.

The teacher wrote on the chalkboard.

1. We enjoyed fire**wood** on the Fourth of July.

2. The plane landed on the **door**way.

3. Rain**coats** fell from the sky.

4. My boots left foot**balls** in the snow.

5. I put my clothes in the **book**case.

6. We woke up at sun**burn**.

7. The fish swam under**ground**.

8. I greeted him with a hand**kerchief**.

Try This! Illustrate two pairs of sentences from above.

© Frank Schaffer Publications, Inc.

Put It Together

Fix the mixed-up puzzle below. First cut the pieces apart. Then arrange the pieces so the words next to each other make the correct compound words. Glue the finished puzzle on another sheet.

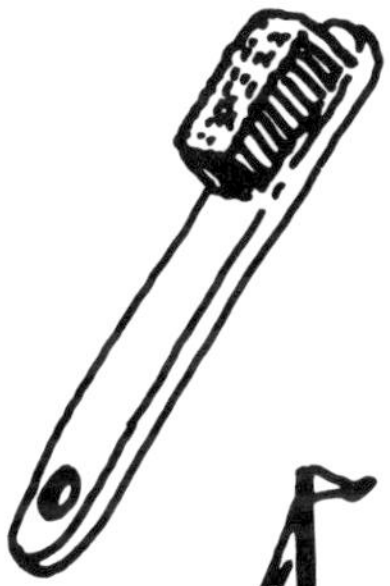

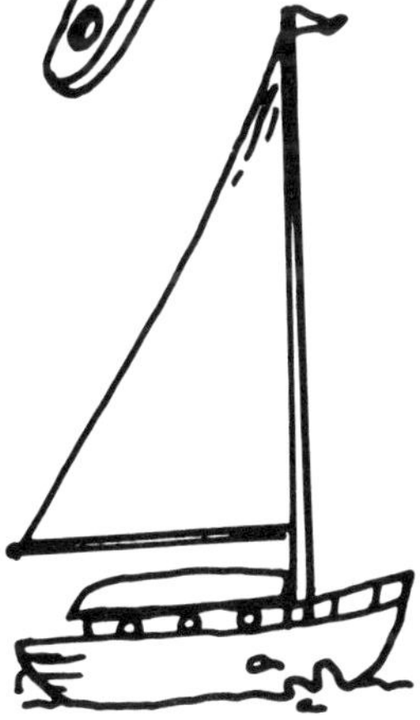

sail, road	plane, fast	boat, air, day
note, bell, tooth	tub, book, birth, bed	room, noon, break
side, door	walk, rail, bath	brush, after

Try This! Make your own puzzle using rhyming words, opposites, or math facts.

© Frank Schaffer Publications, Inc.

Name ______________________________ Skill: Synonyms

Take My Place

Choose the word from the Word Box that could take the place of the boldfaced word in each sentence. Write it on the line.

Word Box

thick whole help choose careful piece

1. I will **select** a new tie for Dad.

2. This box is heavy. Will you **assist** me?

3. Today we saw every animal in the **entire** zoo!

4. I'd like a small **portion** of the cake, please.

5. I didn't see you hiding in those **dense** bushes.

6. Be **cautious** when crossing the street.

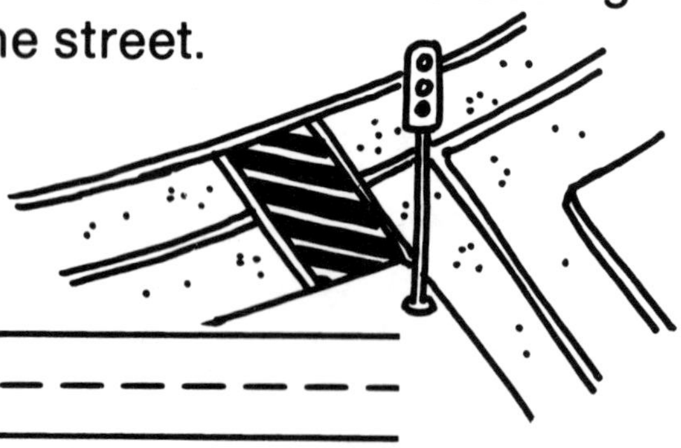

Brainwork! Write five words that could take the place of the word *said*.

Name ____________________ Skill: Synonyms

Figure It Out

Read each sentence. Use the picture clue to help you figure out the meaning of the boldfaced word. Circle the correct meaning. Write it on the line.

1. The workers are **constructing** a new house on our street.

building   moving

2. Our plane **departed** at ten o'clock.

landed   left

3. I waited for Sandy to **reply.**

Dear Sandy,
Can you come to my party on Sunday at 2:00? Let me know.
Your friend,
Keri.

answer   visit

4. The teacher corrected my spelling **error.**

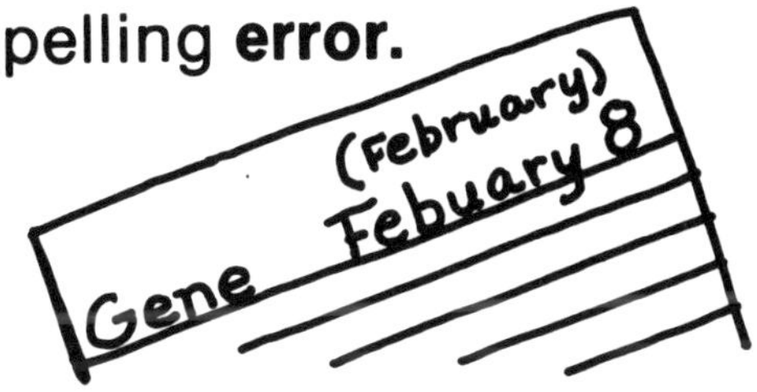

month   mistake

5. Blowing up a balloon **alters** its shape.

changes   colors

6. He will now **demonstrate** how the robot works.

believe   show

Brainwork! List at least five things to which you could *reply.*

© Frank Schaffer Publications, Inc.

Name ______________________________ Skill: Antonyms

Get the Picture

Look at each picture and sentence. One word in the sentence is wrong. Circle the wrong word. Then write the word that would make the sentence true.

1. Pam is surprised because there is something in the box.

____

nothing everything

2. The plane will leave at one o'clock.

____

runway arrive

3. Tim doesn't know that there is a bee on the front of his shirt.

____

sleeve back

4. When you set the table, place the fork on the right side of the plate.

____

left same

5. Kim is sad because she found the missing bunny.

____

tired happy

6. He stayed in bed because he was well.

____

sick young

Brainwork! The words *never* and *always* are opposites. Make a safety poster which has an "always" and a "never" rule.

© Frank Schaffer Publications, Inc.

Name ____________________

I Meant to Say

Each sentence below was meant to say the opposite. Circle the incorrect word in each sentence. Choose a word from the Word Box to replace it. Rewrite the sentence using the new word.

Word Box					
sad	after	hard	odd	apart	borrow

1. I chipped a tooth on the soft candy.

2. Three and five are even numbers.

3. My puzzle pieces fell together.

4. June comes before May.

5. I was happy when my friend moved.

6. May I lend your eraser?

Brainwork! Write each of these words and its opposite: first, began, mean, give, same, young, noise, and always.

© Frank Schaffer Publications, Inc.

M _ ssing Lett _ rs

Dr. Find-it, the word detective, is faced with a puzzling case. It seems that letters are missing from all kinds of words. Her only clue is that the second word in each pair is a synonym or antonym of the first. She's stumped by the case because she has forgotten that a synonym is a word that means almost the same as another word, and an antonym means the opposite. Help Dr. Find-it solve the case by filling in the missing letters.

	Synonym		Antonym
1. c __ p	hat	16. __ ear	far
2. l __ tt __ __	small	17. a __ ov __	below
3. s __ or __	shop	18. __ __ ite	black
4. __ __ in	smile	19. bu __	sell
5. sh __ v __	push	20. w __ __ e	foolish
6. __ __ gin	start	21. __ __ f __	hard
7. __ ll	sick	22. hu __ e	tiny
8. sc __ __ am	yell	23. fr __ __ nd	enemy
9. f __ __	repair	24. tr __ __ h	lie
10. gi __ __	present	25. c __ __ l	warm
11. __ app __	glad	26. __ __ rly	late
12. a __ d	help	27. q __ ie __	loud
13. e __ __ or	mistake	28. l __ __ se	tight
14. we __ __	cry	29. asl __ __ p	awake
15. h __ __ t	stop	30. c __ __ se	open

Try This! Use graph paper to make a word search of synonyms or antonyms.

Name ______________________________ Skill: Homonyms

Which One?

Look at each pair of words in the Word Box. Read the clues carefully to find which word belongs in the puzzle.

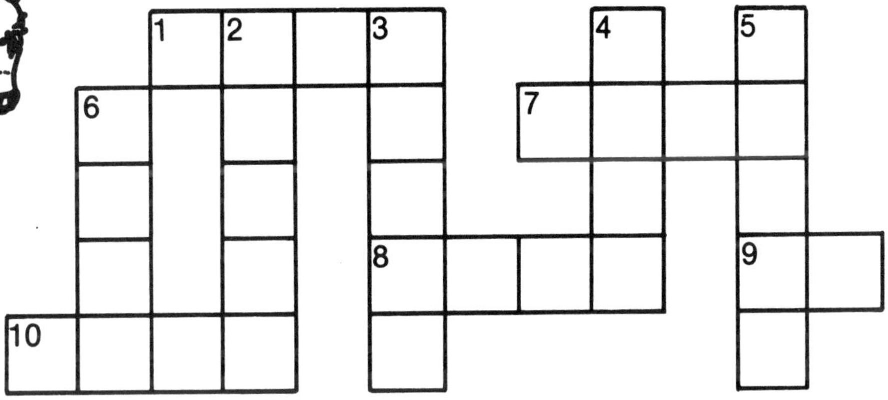

Word Box

sale-sail	whole-hole	sent-cent	pair-pear	our-hour
dear-deer	plane-plain	no-know	write-right	ate-eight

Across

1. an animal with antlers
7. to travel across water
8. 60 minutes of time
9. the opposite of yes
10. a penny

Down

2. the number before nine
3. the opposite of wrong
4. a set of two
5. a flying machine
6. an opening

Brainwork! Write a sentence to show the meaning of the unused word in each pair.

© Frank Schaffer Publications, Inc.

Name ______________________ Skill: Homonyms

The Right Words

Some words sound alike but have different spellings and meanings. Look at the pairs of words in the Word Box. Read the story below. Look for the incorrect words and circle them. Then rewrite the story using the right words.

Word Box				
road	waist	lone	weight	by
rode	waste	loan	wait	buy

Land of His Own

The cowboy road his horse into town. He didn't waist any time getting there. He went to the bank to get a lone. He had to weight awhile. But soon he had money to by land of his own!

Land of His Own

Brainwork! Write a story using one word from each pair of words in the Word Box. Be sure to use the word with the right meaning.

© Frank Schaffer Publications, Inc.

I See What You Mean

wiggle broken

When you read the words *wiggle* or *broken* above, you can almost see their meanings. You can show the meanings of some words by the way you write the letters.

Read each word below. Use special letters to write the word in a way that shows its meaning.

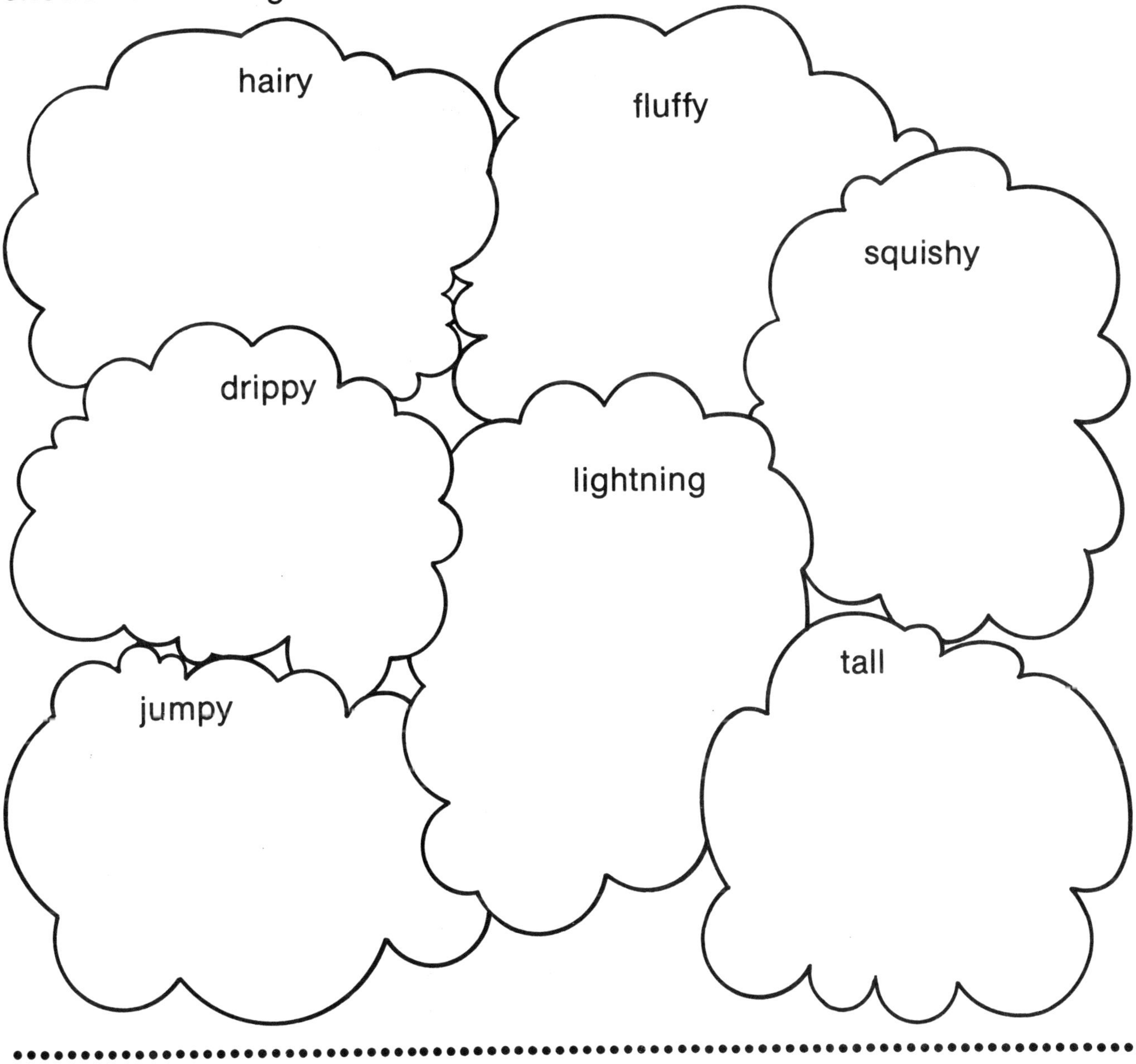
hairy
fluffy
squishy
drippy
lightning
tall
jumpy

Try This! Write three sentences in which at least one of the words is written in a way that shows its meaning. Example: I saw a FAT worm.

© Frank Schaffer Publications, Inc.

Name ____________________ Skill: Pronoun referents

Good Sports

Bill and Sara are brother and sister. They are on the same soccer team. Sara is an excellent kicker. **She**[1] scores many goals. Bill is a terrific goalie. Many times **he**[2] keeps the other team from scoring. Bill and Sara often hear their parents cheering **them**[3] on. They say **it**[4] helps them play their best. They don't always win the game, but **both**[5] always enjoy **it.**[6]

Each numbered word in the story stands for the name of someone or something in the story. Decide what each word replaces. Write your answers on the lines below.

1. She— ____________________
   Bill Sara
2. He— ____________________
   Bill Sara
3. them— ____________________
   Bill and Sara Bill and Sara's parents
4. it— ____________________
   scoring cheering
5. both— ____________________
   Bill and Sara Bill and Sara's parents
6. it— ____________________
   winning the game

Brainwork! What sport do you enjoy playing or watching? Write about it.

© Frank Schaffer Publications, Inc.

Name______________________________ Skill: Word patterns—final e

Pattern Pairs

Write the correct word from each pair to complete each sentence.

1. There is a ________ tree in the yard.	pin
2. You can hold cloth together with a ________.	pine
3. I need a ________ of cloth.	scrap
4. I got a ________ when I fell.	scrape
5. The ________ puppy wanted to play.	cut
6. I ________ the paper in half.	cute
7. The bird likes to ________ on the window.	tap
8. Use ________ to hold up the sign.	tape
9. The apple was ________.	rip
10. I got a ________ in my new jacket.	ripe
11. We ________ to take a trip there.	plan
12. Grandpa came on a ________.	plane

Brainwork! Choose a pair of sentences above to copy and illustrate.

© Frank Schaffer Publications, Inc.

Name

Seeing Double

The words in each list contain double letters. Use the clues to complete the words.
Write the missing letters on the blanks.

_ _ l l	filled up
_ _ l l	not sharp
_ _ l l _	sweet bread spread
_ _ l l _ _	type of money
_ _ l l _ _	on your shirt
_ _ l l _ _	between mountains
_ _ l l _ _ _	a large number
_ _ _ _ l l _	found on a beach
_ _ l l _ _ _	filled with air

_ o o _ _	in your mouth
_ o o _	seen at night
_ _ _ _ o o _	a place to learn
_ o o _ _	not tight
_ o o _	a horse's foot
_ _ o o _ _	make a choice
_ _ o o _	holds thread
_ _ o o _ _	not rough
_ o o _	what we eat

_ _ e e _	a color	_ _ e e _ _	a soft wind
_ _ _ e e	after two	_ e e _	not shallow
_ _ e e _	king's wife	_ _ e e _	where legs bend
_ _ e e _	put on a bed	_ _ _ e e _ _	hold tightly

Try This! Pick a pair of double letters such as *rr*, *ss*, *dd*, or *tt*. Make a "Seeing Double" puzzle for a friend to solve.

© Frank Schaffer Publications, Inc.

Getting In Shape

Write each word from the Word List in the shape where it belongs.

Clothing

Word List

train
Jefferson
coat
New York
pine
Reagan
bus
oak
Texas
dress
ship
shirt
plane
California
Lincoln
apple
palm
pants
Kennedy
Florida

Trees

Presidents

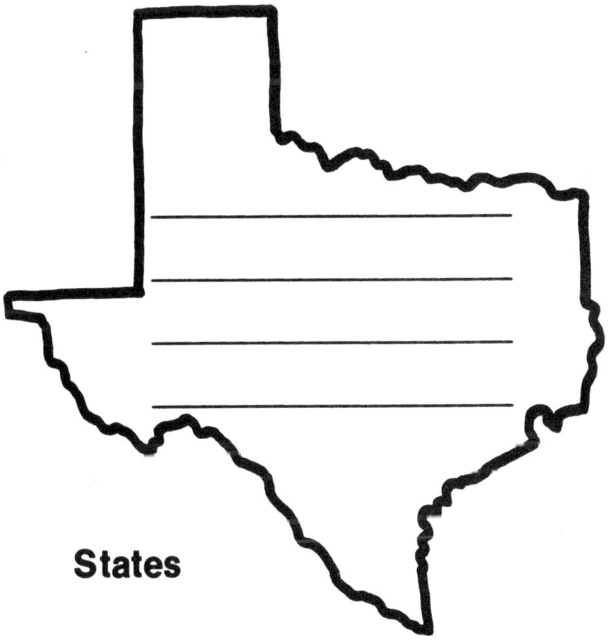

States

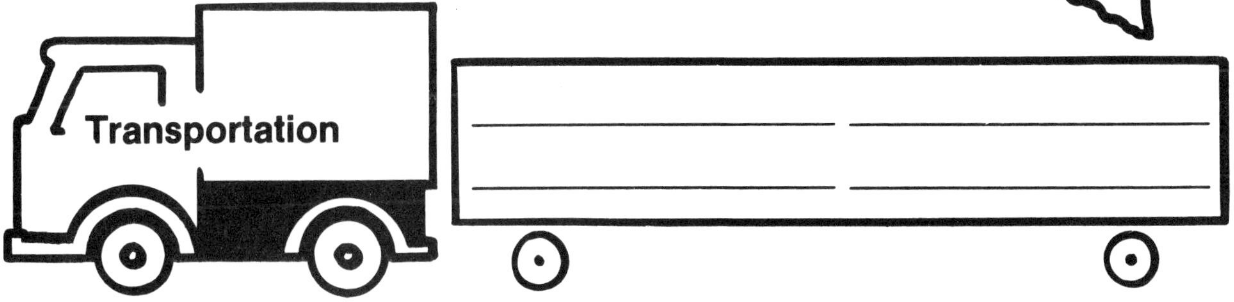
Transportation

Try This! Draw another category shape. Write five words inside.

© Frank Schaffer Publications, Inc.

Name

Start With a Vowel

Begin with a vowel and add a letter to each line to make a new word. The new letter may be added to the beginning, middle, or end of the word above it. There is a clue beside the new word to help you.

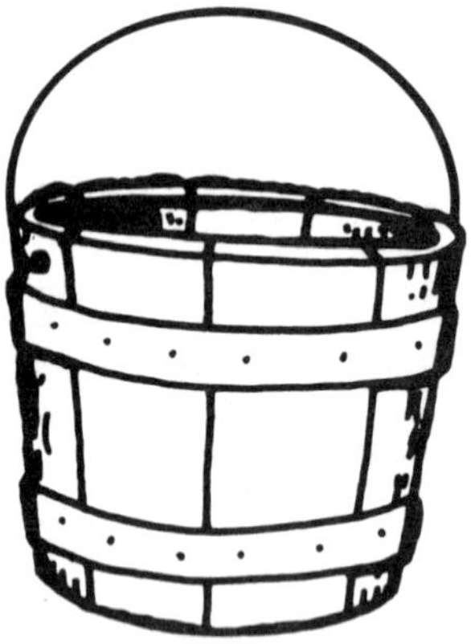

1) **a**
__ __ (dad)
__ __ __ (friend)
__ __ __ __ (bucket)

2) **e**
__ __ (myself)
__ __ __ (opposite of women)
__ __ __ __ (cruel)

3) **i**
__ __ (hello)
__ __ __ (part of body above the leg)
__ __ __ __ (boat)

4) **o**
__ __ (opposite of yes)
__ __ __ (present time)
__ __ __ __ (flakes of ice)

5) **u**
__ __ (opposite of down)
__ __ __ (young dog)
__ __ __ __ (machine that supplies gasoline)

6) **y**
__ __ (belongs to me)
__ __ __ (name of a month)
__ __ __ __ (a lot)

Try This! Make your own word puzzle. Share it with a friend.

Word Towers

Each word tower in this castle is made by adding one letter to the beginning or end of a word to make the next word. Use the clues to help you complete each word tower. Write one letter in each blank.

Example:
i n not out
p i n used to fasten
s p i n turn around
1.
_ _ _ had eaten
_ _ _ _ not early
_ _ _ _ _ used to serve food
2.
_ _ _ _ falling water
_ _ _ _ _ runs on tracks
_ _ _ _ _ _ filter
3.
myself _ _
grown boys _ _ _
fix _ _ _ _
4.
think ahead _ _ _ _
aircraft _ _ _ _ _
heavenly body _ _ _ _ _ _

Try This! Build your own word tower with clues for a friend to solve.

© Frank Schaffer Publications, Inc.

Name

Picture Perfect

Color the design below by following these directions.

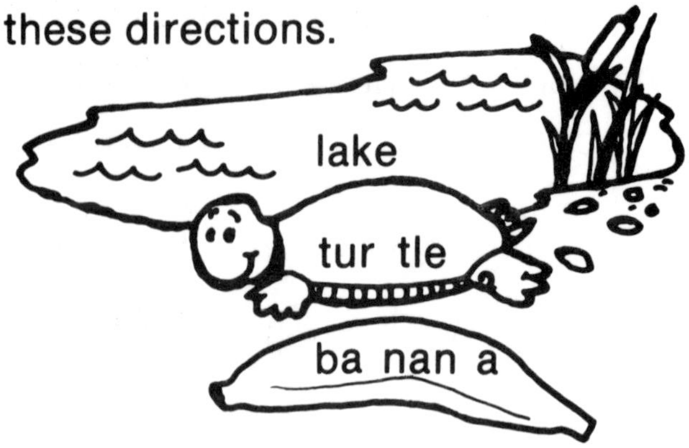
lake
tur tle
ba nan a

Color one-syllable words blue.

Color two-syllable words green.

Color three-syllable words yellow.

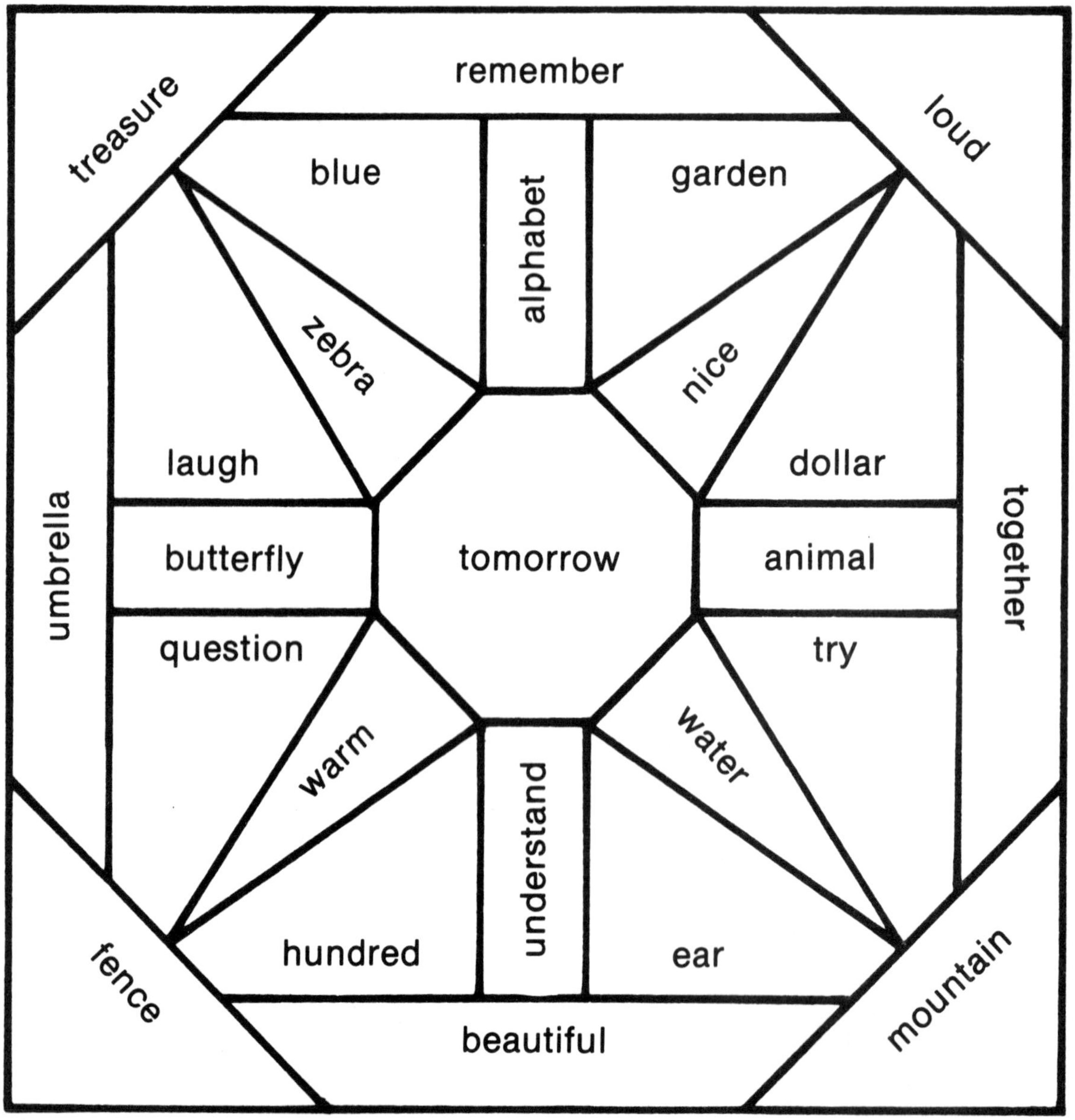
remember
treasure
loud
blue
alphabet
garden
zebra
nice
laugh
dollar
umbrella
butterfly
tomorrow
animal
together
question
try
warm
water
understand
hundred
ear
fence
mountain
beautiful

Try This! Draw your own design. Make a new puzzle for a friend to color.

© Frank Schaffer Publications, Inc.

Forward and Backward

To solve each puzzle below, use the clues to discover a special pair of words. The second word is the first word *backwards!*

a number word ten
used to catch fish net

1
used for frying p _ _
a short sleep n _ _

2
right away n _ _
finished first in a race w _ _

3
not all p _ _ _
catch and hold t _ _ _

4
animals to keep p _ _ _
put your foot on s _ _ _

5
friend p _ _
appears when you sit l _ _

6
swallow hard g _ _ _
at the end of a wire p _ _ _

7
shines at night s _ _ _
small furry animals r _ _ _

8
crunchy to eat n _ _ _
sudden shock s _ _ _

Try This! Some words are spelled the same forward and backward like the word *dad.* Think of three or more words like this. Write them.

Name ________________ Skill: Commonly misused words

Which Is It?

Look at each pair of words below. They look almost the same but they have different meanings. Choose the correct word for each sentence. Fill in the ○ above the word.

metal—shiny, hard material **medal**—an award	**through**—in one side and out the other **thorough**—complete	**then**—at that time **than**—a comparison

1. Mom told me to do a ______ job of cleaning my room.

○ through ○ thorough

2. The dog barked, ______ he wagged his tail.

○ then ○ than

3. I got a ______ for first place in the contest.

○ medal ○ metal

4. The railroad track went ______ a long tunnel.

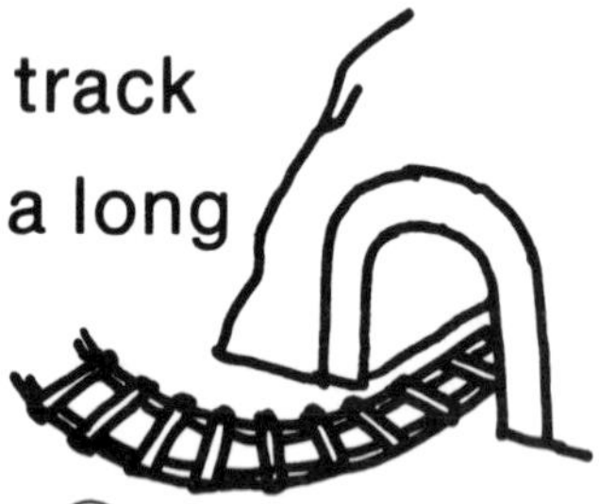

○ through ○ thorough

5. My new bike is bigger ______ my old one.

○ then ○ than

6. The tent was made of cloth with ______ poles.

○ medal ○ metal

Brainwork! Use each pair of words in a sentence. Example: I used to be shorter **than** my sister, but **then** I grew!

Name ______________________ Skill: Commonly misused words

Not Quite

Some words look very much alike but have different meanings. Look at the words and their meanings below. Then choose the correct word for each sentence. Fill in the ◯ above the word and write it on the line.

quite—very **quiet**—not noisy	**loose**—not tight **lose**—misplace	**guest**—visitor **guessed**—made a guess

1. We had a ______________ for dinner.

◯ guest ◯ guessed

4. The weather was ______________ hot yesterday.

◯ quite ◯ quiet

2. I promise not to ______________ the note.

◯ loose ◯ lose

5. The children ______________ who was behind the mask.

◯ guest ◯ guessed

3. The children kept ______________ during the fire drill.

◯ quite ◯ quiet

6. My tooth was ______________ so I didn't want to eat an apple.

◯ lose ◯ loose

Brainwork! "I **guessed** we were having a **guest.**" Write sentences using the other two pairs of words from the Word Box.

© Frank Schaffer Publications, Inc.

Name ______________________ Skill: Commonly misused words

A Close Call

Look at the words and meanings below. Choose the correct word to complete each sentence. Then write the meaning of the word you chose on the line below the sentence.

desert—very dry land

dessert—after-meal treat

1. Dad made us pudding for a special ____________.

2. We drove across miles of sandy ____________.

lose—misplace

loose—not tight

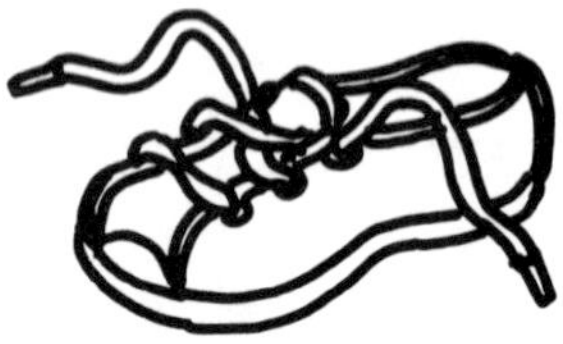

3. My brother's sweater was too ____________.

4. The money is in my pocket so I won't ____________ it.

single—only, one

signal— warning sign

5. The ____________ letter in the mailbox was for me.

6. The red light was a ____________ to stop.

Brainwork! What can't you do with a door? Clothes it! Write two riddles like this using the words **picture** and **pitcher.**

© Frank Schaffer Publications, Inc.

Name

Secret Color Code

Reading and writing coded messages is fun. To read or decode this message, circle the words that come after colors. Then write the circled words on the line below the message.

My yellow Meet work red me elephant pink in the seven hamburger blue the school purple park cow.

Use these three easy steps to write or encode a message.

1. Write the message leaving large spaces between the words.

Example: I like you

2. Write a color before each of the words in the message.

Example: orange I green like brown you

3. Fill in the rest of the blank spaces with other words.

Example: Can orange I bicycle the green like shoes desk work secret flowers brown you zoo television bus now.

Write your own message using the secret color code.

Try This! Switch with a friend and decode each other's message.

© Frank Schaffer Publications, Inc.

Name ____________________

Directions:

- ☐ Draw a line to match each picture and word.
- ☐ Underline the vowel in each word.
- ☐ Circle the two words that rhyme.
- ☐ Make a box around the longest word.

cap

kick

man

cup

dog

pick

ships

pig

Name ______________________________

Directions:

☐ Match the words in the box to make a new word.

☐ Write the new words.

☐ Draw a picture for each word.

☐ Number the words in abc order (write the number in the ○).

base	news	flash	tooth	sun
paper	brush	ball	flower	light

Words	Pictures
○	
○	
○	
○	
○	

Name ____

Directions: In each row:

- ☐ Circle words with the same vowel sound.
- ☐ Underline the word that rhymes with the first word.
- ☐ Find a rhyming word that fits into each word shape below.
- ☐ Write the rhyming words in the correct shape.

1. cat	rat	sand	rip	and
2. red	leg	bed	egg	saw
3. fun	fan	sun	hut	lift
4. lip	kite	wig	fin	drip
5. hot	rod	slot	on	hope

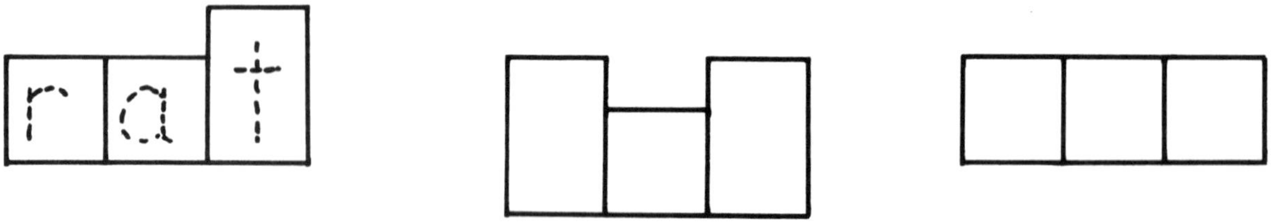

© Frank Schaffer Publications, Inc.

Name ____________________

Directions:

☐ Write a word in each shape. Check off the words as you use them.

☐ Read the sentences.

☐ Write the number of the missing word.

Words to use

1. write
2. friend
3. basket
4. bicycle
5. under
6. ready

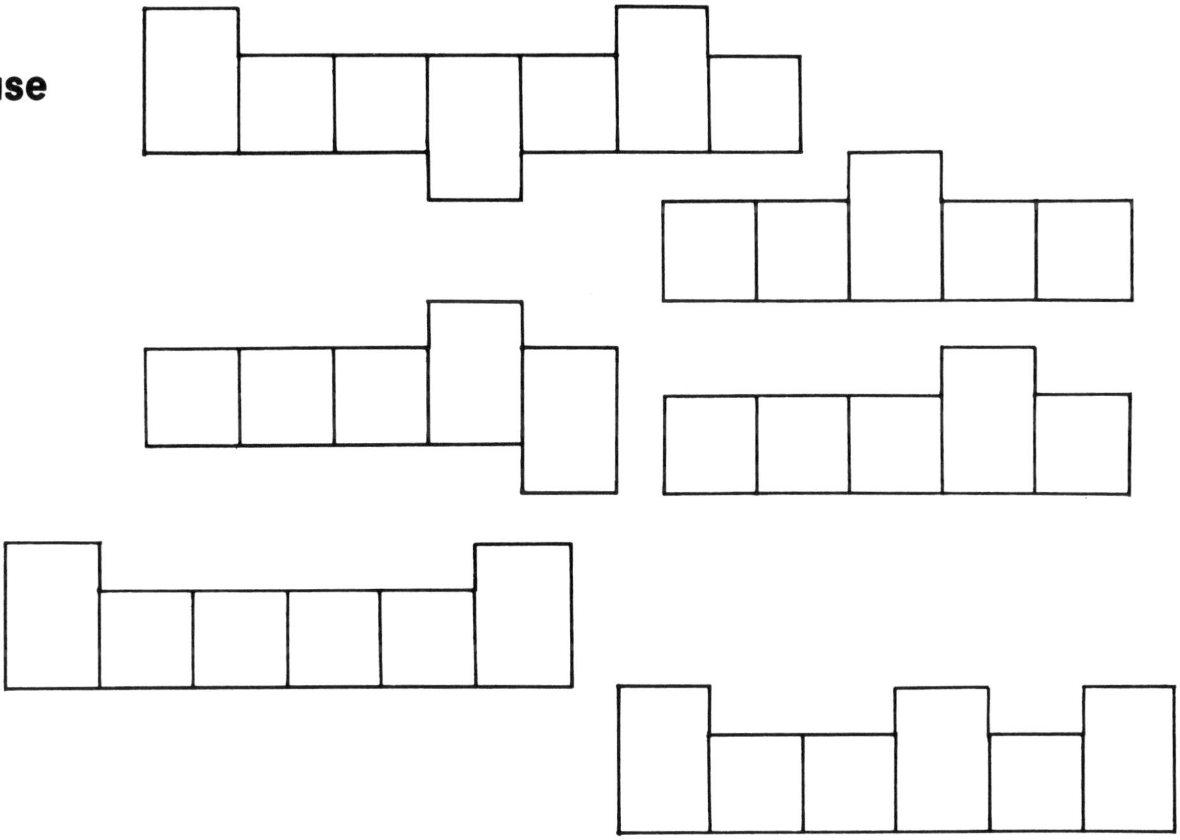

Sentences

Kim is my best _____ .

I found the book _____ my bed.

Are you _____ to start?

Put the apples in the _____ .

Did you ride your _____ today?

_____ your name on your paper.

© Frank Schaffer Publications, Inc.

Name ______________________________

Directions:

☐ Fill in the missing letters on the chart.

*	A	B	C	*
D	______	F	G	______
I	______	______	L	M
N	O	______	______	R
S	______	U	V	______
*	X	______	Z	*

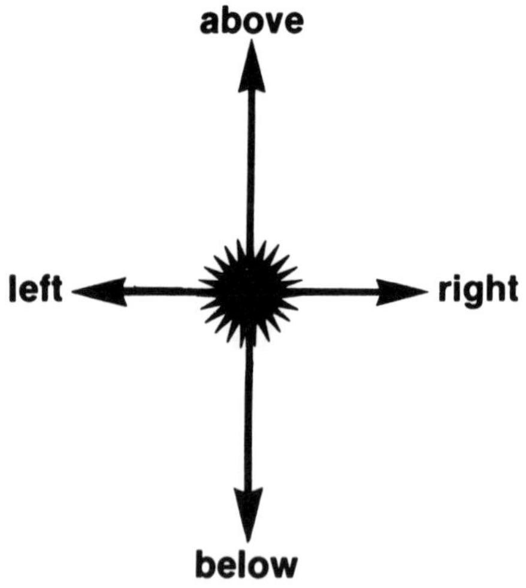
above
left
right
below

______ ______ ______ ______ ______ ______ ______
1 2 3 4 5 6 7

☐ On ______ (1) write the seventh letter of the alphabet.
☐ On ______ (6) write the letter before G.
☐ On ______ (3) write the letter to the right of Q.
☐ On ______ (2) write the letter below D on the chart.
☐ On ______ (7) write the letter to the right of D.
☐ On ______ (5) write the letter to the left of G.
☐ On ______ (4) write the letter above E.

© Frank Schaffer Publications, Inc.

Name ________________________________

Directions:

☐ Fill in the missing numbers on the number chart.

☐ Write the numbers 1 to 12 on clock #1.

☐ Write the numbers I to XII (Roman Numerals) on clock #2.

☐ Draw an hour hand on clock #1. Make the clock say 5 o'clock.

☐ Draw an hour hand on clock #2. Make the clock say 8 o'clock.

Number Chart

1	___	___	4	___	6	___	___	___	10	___	12
I	II	III	IV	V	VI	VII	VIII	IX	X	XI	XII

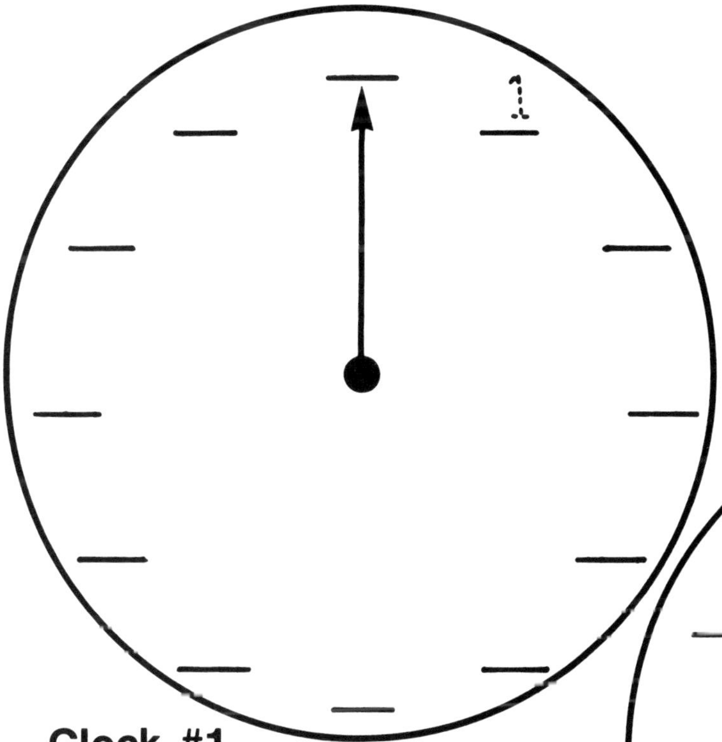

Clock #1

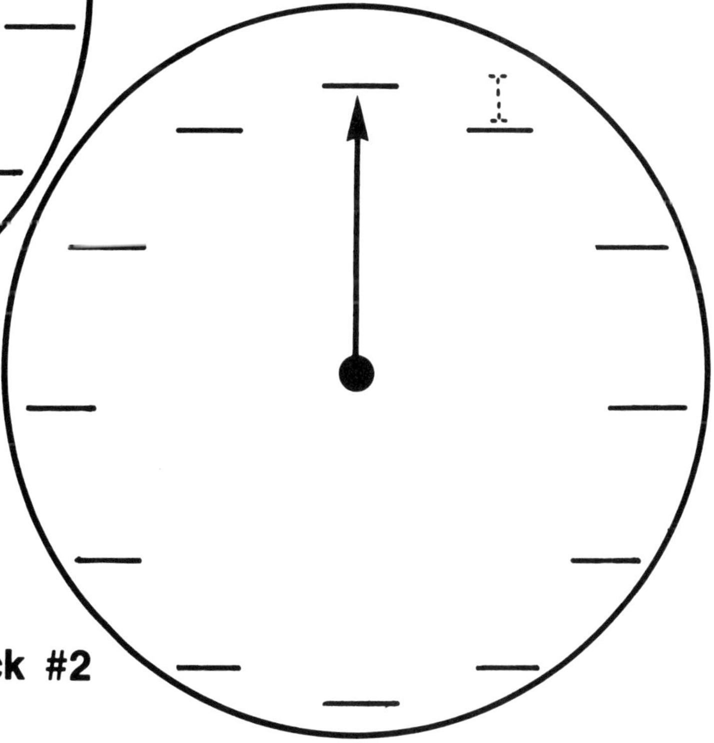

Clock #2

© Frank Schaffer Publications, Inc.

Name ____________________

Directions:

- ☐ Use a letter from the box to complete each word.
- ☐ Cross out the letter that you used.
- ☐ On the _ _ _ write a word with the three letters you have left.
- ☐ In the ☐ draw a picture to go with the word.

b__i__ke 

shi____ 

ro____e 

co____e 

ska____e 

s____ck 

b____s 

____ook 

____ake 

____ ____ ____ ☐

t	i
u	b
n	o
p	s
n	c
u	s

© Frank Schaffer Publications, Inc.

Name ______________________________

Directions:

☐ Use the chart to fill in dates on the calendar.

☐ Fill in all the missing numbers up to 31.

Row	Day	Date
X	Tuesday	18
●	Saturday	15
▲	Saturday	1
◆	Thursday	6
▮	Friday	28
+	Sunday	30
◆	Monday	3
X	Wednesday	19

	Sunday	Monday	Tuesday	Wednesday	Thursday	Friday	Saturday
▲	____	____	____	____	____	____	____
◆	____	____	____	____	____	____	____
●	____	____	____	____	____	____	____
X	____	____	18	____	____	____	____
▮	____	____	____	____	____	____	____
+	____	____	____	____	____	____	____

Name ______________________________

Directions:

- ☐ Mark the ○ to show the answers in box #1
- ☐ In box #2 mark ☺ if word is spelled correctly,
  ☹ if word is spelled wrong.

#1

6+2	6 ○	8 ○	4 ○
7+1	8 ○	7 ○	9 ○
4–0	0 ○	4 ○	1 ○
5–3	8 ○	6 ○	2 ○
2+2	4 ○	2 ○	1 ○
6+0	0 ○	6 ○	5 ○
4+1	5 ○	6 ○	3 ○
7–2	3 ○	5 ○	7 ○

#2

	pig	☺ ○	☹ ○		bed	☺ ○	☹ ○
	tup	☺ ○	☹ ○		dosh	☺ ○	☹ ○
	fish	☺ ○	☹ ○		dob	☺ ○	☹ ○

© Frank Schaffer Publications, Inc.

Name ____________________

Directions:

☐ Color one big ◯ red.
☐ Color one big ◯ blue.
☐ Color one big ◯ yellow.
☐ With purple, color the small circle between red and blue.
☐ With green, color the small circle between blue and yellow.
☐ With orange, color the small circle between yellow and red.
☐ Fill in the **Color Chart** to show how to make colors. Choose two to make each color.

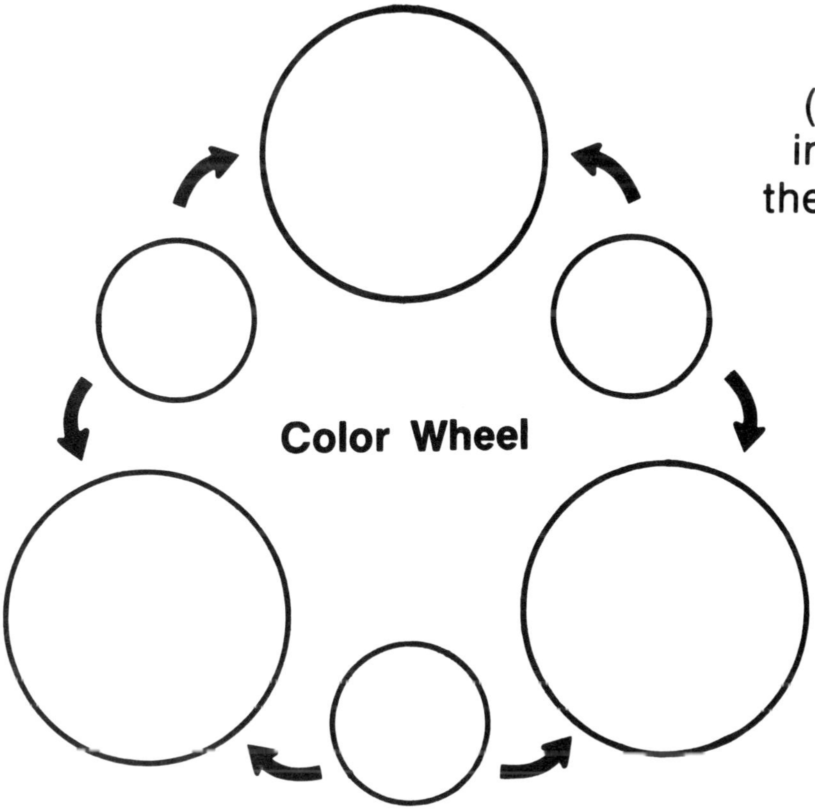

Color Wheel

(To make the colors in the small ◯ use the color on each side.)

Color Chart

To Make	**Mix** Red	Blue	Yellow
Orange	◯	◯	◯
Green	◯	◯	◯
Purple	◯	◯	◯

© Frank Schaffer Publications, Inc.

Name ______________________________

Directions: Use the words in the box.

☐ Circle the number words.

☐ Draw a line under the color words.

☐ Put a box around the animal words.

☐ Draw a line through all other words.

☐ Count and fill in the chart.

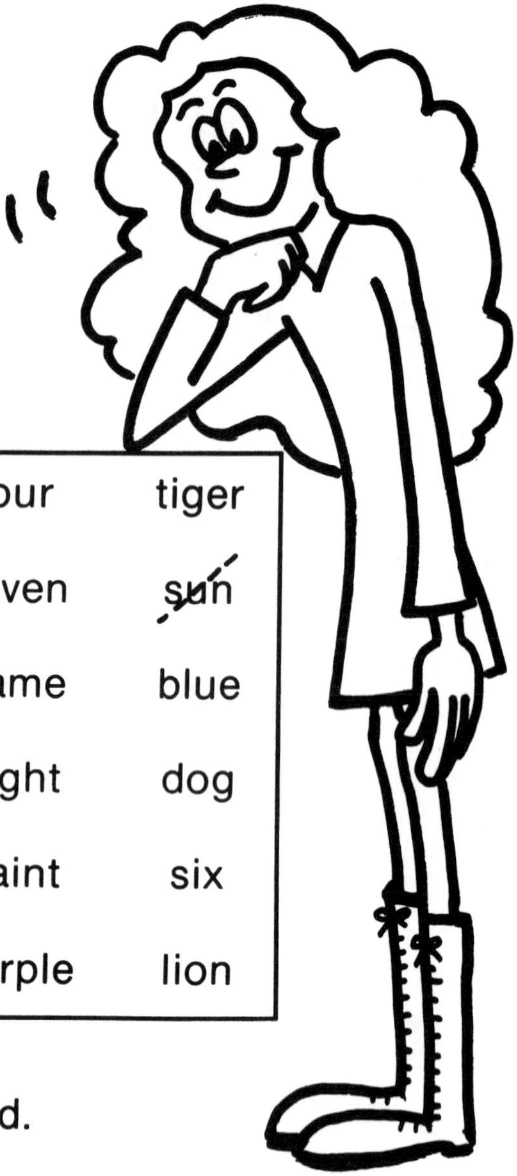

one	cat	black	four	tiger
red	mouse	zero	seven	sun
ten	lunch	two	game	blue
white	hat	rat	eight	dog
horse	teacher	yellow	paint	six
green	three	funny	purple	lion

Chart—Color one ☐ for each word.

Kinds of words	**How many?**									**Total**
Number words										
Color words										
Animal words										
Other words										

© Frank Schaffer Publications, Inc.

Name ____

Directions:

☐ Draw a line under the numbers you use to count by fives.

☐ Circle the numbers you use to count by tens.

☐ Draw a box around the number that is the same as your age.

1	2	3	4	5	6	7	8	9	10	11	12
13	14	15	16	17	18	19	20	21	22	23	24
25	26	27	28	29	30	31	32	33	34	35	36
37	38	39	40	41	42	43	44	45	46	47	48
49	50	51	52	53	54	55	56	57	58	59	60
61	62	63	64	65	66	67	68	69	70	71	72
73	74	75	76	77	78	79	80	81	82	83	84
85	86	87	88	89	90	91	92	93	94	95	96
97	98	99	100								

Name ______________________________

Directions:

- ☐ Write words from the box on the chart.
- ☐ Check off the words as you write them.
- ☐ Count the words in each list. Write the number in the last box in each row.
- ☐ Answer the questions below the chart.

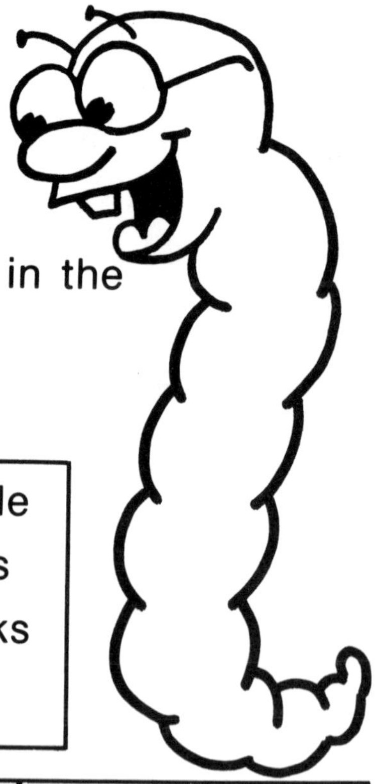

✓bike	game	coat	cards	apple
hat	meat	car	shirt	bus
cookie	shoes	ball	cheese	socks
jeans	train	bread	jet	

To Eat	To Wear	To Play	To Ride
			bike
How Many?			

Questions (color the ○ to show the answer):

Which list has:	**Eat**	**Wear**	**Play**	**Ride**
1. the most words	○	○	○	○
2. the least words	○	○	○	○
3. the same amount	○	○	○	○

Name ______________________________

Directions: Fill in the _____ with north, south, east or west.

- ☐ The kangaroo is __________ of the monkeys.
- ☐ Snakes are __________ of the birds.
- ☐ Tigers are __________ of the seals.
- ☐ The parking lot is __________ of the gorilla.
- ☐ Seals are __________ of the gorilla and kangaroo.
- ☐ Lions are __________ of the bears.
- ☐ Make two cars and one bus in the parking lot.

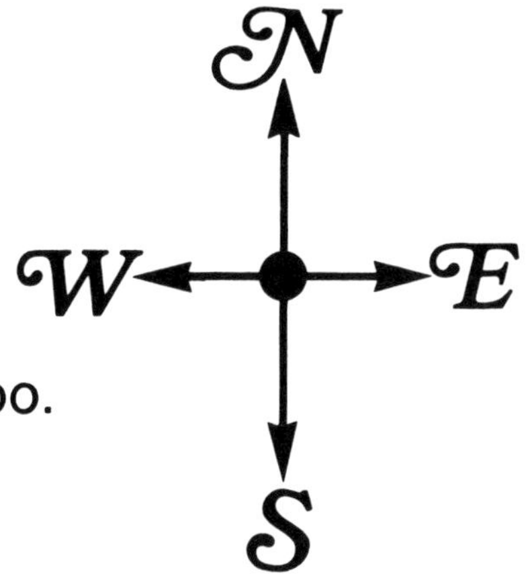
N
W
E
S

Parking Lot
Gorilla
Kangaroo
Seals
Lions
Bears
Monkeys
Tigers
Snakes
Birds

Name ______________________________

Directions: In each row mark the problem with the correct answer.

1	5 + 4 = 8 ○	9 − 2 = 7 ○	9 − 7 = 3 ○
2	7 − 5 = 3 ○	4 + 2 = 7 ○	7 − 7 = 0 ○
3	10 + 0 = 10 ○	8 − 6 = 3 ○	5 + 4 = 8 ○
4	6 + 5 = 12 ○	5 + 3 = 8 ○	9 + 2 = 10 ○
5	2 + 6 = 9 ○	11 − 5 = 7 ○	12 − 7 = 5 ○
6	5 + 4 = 9 ○	7 + 2 = 5 ○	9 − 7 = 3 ○
7	12 − 6 = 5 ○	6 + 7 = 9 ○	6 − 0 = 6 ○
8	8 − 7 = 2 ○	8 − 8 = 0 ○	6 + 4 = 8 ○
9	5 − 4 = 9 ○	4 − 2 = 2 ○	9 − 5 = 3 ○
10	12 − 3 = 9 ○	9 + 2 = 12 ○	7 + 4 = 10 ○
11	8 + 0 = 0 ○	9 − 5 = 3 ○	8 − 8 = 0 ○

Name ______________________________

Directions: Mark the ○ to show the correct answer.

Sound	Picture	Answer	Sound	Picture	Answer
middle		s ○ n ○ u ○	beginning		g ○ d ○ t ○
ending		t ○ d ○ c ○	middle		p ○ u ○ a ○
beginning		h ○ t ○ d ○	ending		g ○ l ○ p ○
ending		ch ○ sh ○ th ○	beginning		c ○ n ○ t ○
middle		i ○ a ○ u ○	middle		a ○ e ○ f ○
ending		h ○ n ○ d ○	ending		m ○ n ○ a ○
beginning		i ○ e ○ g ○	beginning		n ○ e ○ m ○
middle		a ○ o ○ e ○	middle		e ○ i ○ w ○
beginning		s ○ z ○ d ○	beginning		sp ○ sh ○ st ○
ending		k ○ g ○ o ○	middle		i ○ w ○ e ○

© Frank Schaffer Publications, Inc.

Name ______________________________

Directions:

☐ Draw a line under the number one less than 54.
☐ Draw a line under the number one greater than ten.
☐ Draw a line under the number one greater than 92.
☐ Draw a line under the number one less than 80.
☐ Draw a line under the number one less than 48.
☐ Draw a line under the number one greater than two.

☐ Put an **X** on the numbers you use to count by twos.

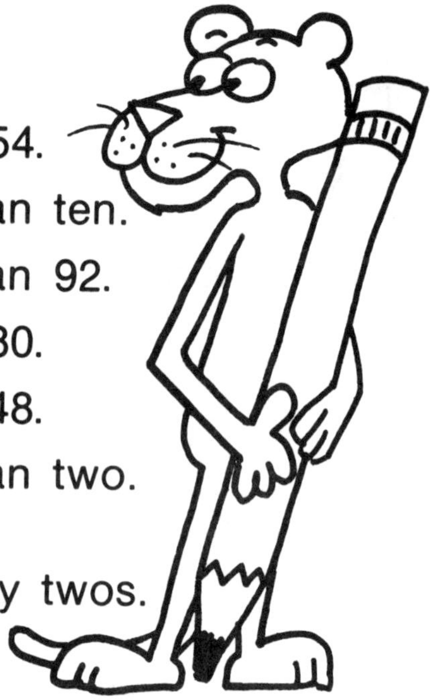

1	2	3	4	5	6	7	8	9	10	11	12
13	14	15	16	17	18	19	20	21	22	23	24
25	26	27	28	29	30	31	32	33	34	35	36
37	38	39	40	41	42	43	44	45	46	47	48
49	50	51	52	53	54	55	56	57	58	59	60
61	62	63	64	65	66	67	68	69	70	71	72
73	74	75	76	77	78	79	80	81	82	83	84
85	86	87	88	89	90	91	92	93	94	95	96
97	98	99	100								

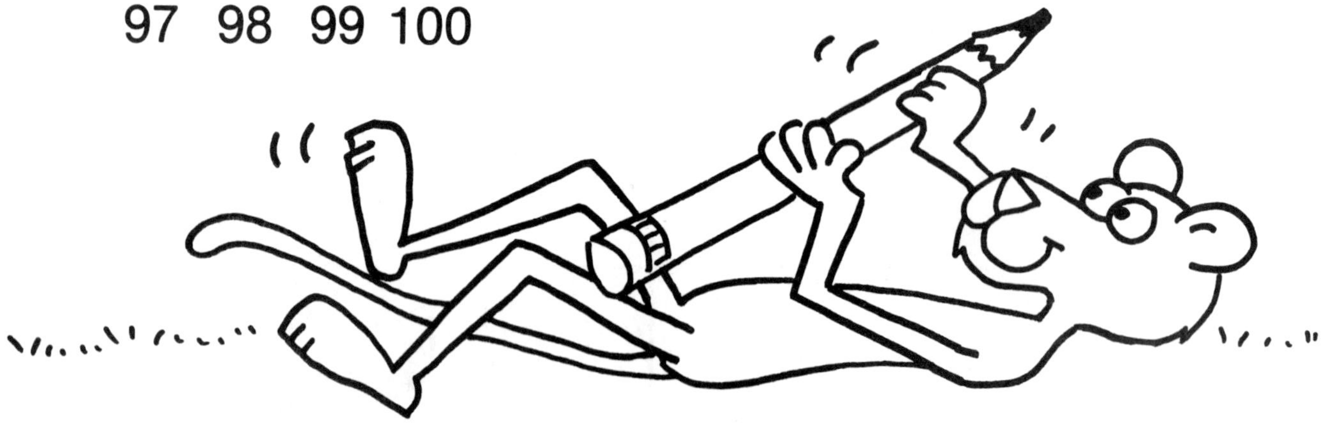

© Frank Schaffer Publications, Inc.

Name ______________________________

Directions:

- ☐ Look at Box 1.
- ☐ On the grid, find **Start** ★.
- ☐ Count over → 1 and up ↑ 2.
- ☐ Put a dot on the grid where you stopped.
- ☐ Write the correct letter by the dot.
- ☐ Go back to **Start** ★.
- ☐ Looking at Box 1, do the rest of the dots and letters on the grid.
- ☐ Draw lines to connect all the dots using Box 2.
- ☐ Color the shape.

Box 1

over →	up ↑	Write
1	2	A
4	5	B
6	7	C
8	5	D
11	2	E
6	2	F

Box 2

Draw a line from:
A to B
B to C
C to D
D to E
E to F
F to A

Grid

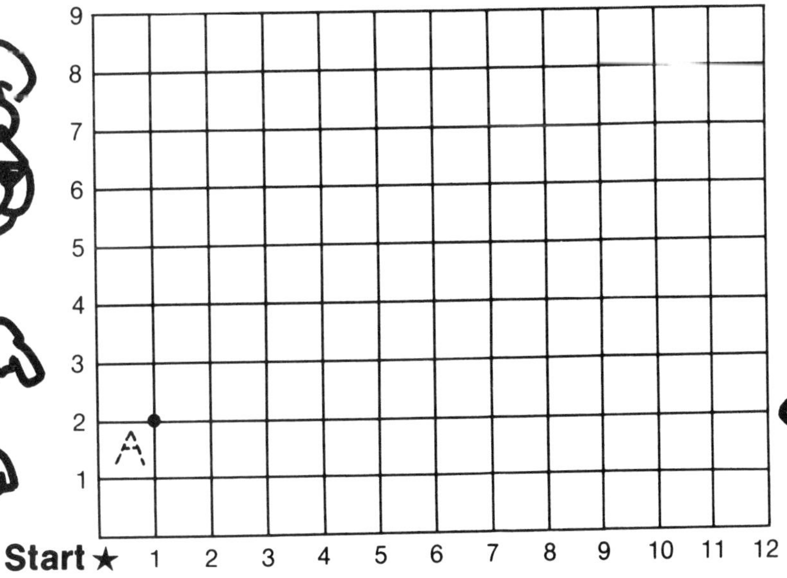

9
8
7
6
5
4
3
2
1
A
Start ★
1 2 3 4 5 6 7 8 9 10 11 12

© Frank Schaffer Publications, Inc.

Name ______________________________

Directions:

- ☐ Look at Box 1.
- ☐ On the grid, find **Start** ★.
- ☐ Count over → 6 and up ↑ 1.
- ☐ Put a dot on the grid where you stopped.
- ☐ Write correct letter by the dot.
- ☐ Go back to **Start** ★.
- ☐ Looking at Box 1, do the rest of the dots and letters on the grid.
- ☐ Draw lines to connect all the dots using Box 2.
- ☐ Color the shape.

Box 1

over →	up ↑	Write
6	1	A
5	4	B
2	5	C
5	6	D
6	9	E
7	6	F
10	5	G
7	4	H

Box 2

Draw a line from:	
A to B	E to F
B to C	F to G
C to D	G to H
D to E	H to A

Grid

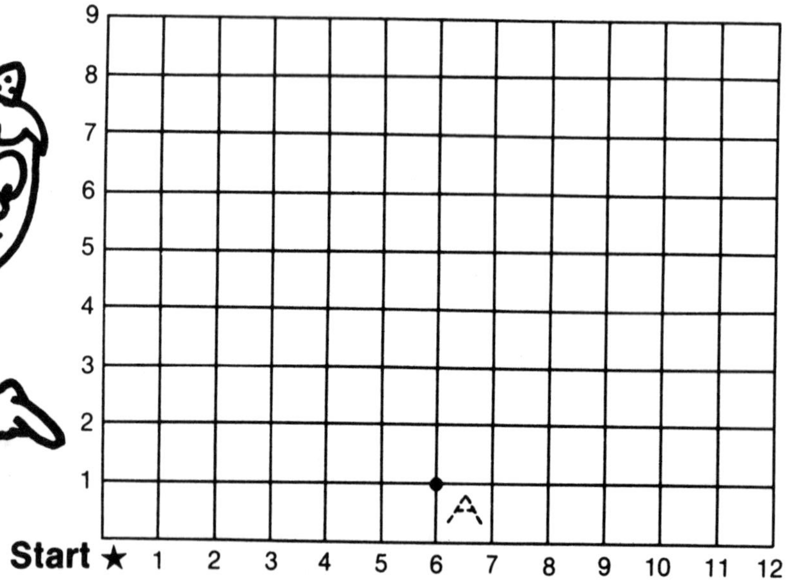
9
8
7
6
5
4
3
2
1
A
Start ★
1 2 3 4 5 6 7 8 9 10 11 12

© Frank Schaffer Publications, Inc.

Name ______________________________

Directions:

☐ Fill in the chart to show how many to count. across → and up ↑ to make the  .

☐ Fill in the letters that tell where to draw lines to make the  .

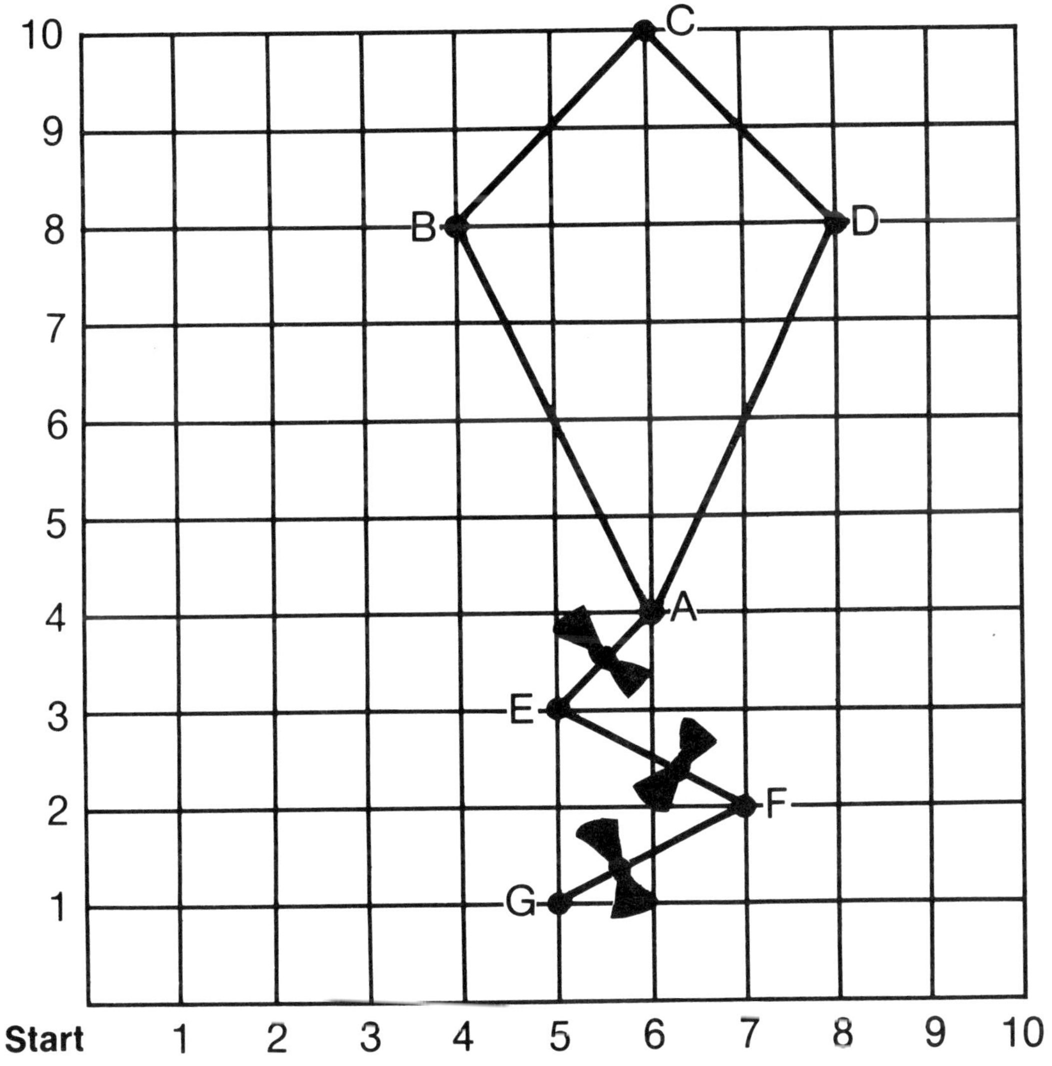

across →	up ↑	Write
6	4	A

Draw a line from:

A to ___

___ to C

___ to D

D to A

A to ___

E to ___

F to ___

© Frank Schaffer Publications, Inc.

Name

What's It Worth?

a 1	b 3	c 3	d 2	e 1	f 2	g 3	h 2	i 1	j 4	k 4	l 2	m 2
n 2	o 1	p 2	q 5	r 2	s 2	t 2	u 1	v 4	w 3	x 5	y 3	z 5

Each letter above is worth from one to five points. Add the points for each letter to find out what a word is worth.

1. Which season is worth 11 points?

____

2. Which month is worth 10 points?

____

3. Which planet is worth 9 points?

____

4. Which color is worth 10 points?

____

5. Which state is worth 15 points?

____

6. Which ball game is worth 21 points?

____

Word Box

summer
winter

July
June

Earth
Uranus

pink
purple

Arizona
Arkansas

baseball
basketball

Try This! How many points is your first name worth? How many points is your last name worth? Which is worth more—your first or last name? How much more?

© Frank Schaffer Publications, Inc.

Name ____________________

Read the stories very carefully. Think about the **main idea** of each one. Circle the **best** answer.

---

1. My dad is a fireman. He helps to put out fires in buildings and houses. Sometimes he works all night long. He is very brave.

a. How to be brave b. My dad's job c. A big tall building

---

2. Think of the things you can find in a book. There are words and pictures, people and places. If you want to know something, look it up in a book.

a. Thinking about people
b. Learning new words
c. What to find in a book

---

3. I live in a yellow and white house. A fence goes all around it. There is a birdhouse hanging in the big green tree. There are many flowers in the garden.

a. A bird taking a bath b. Going for a walk c. A story about my house

---

4. We have a dog named Moose. Moose likes to eat. Sometimes he eats three lunches and four dinners. Now he is so big he can't fit into his house. Only his head will fit through the door. My dad says we will have to build a barn for Moose to live in.

a. A late night dinner
b. Houses that are small
c. The dog who eats too much

Thinking Time

Read the next 2 questions carefully. Then answer them on the back of this paper.

5. Name a job that you would like to have. Describe the job.

6. The fourth story tells about a dog that ate too much. Sometimes people eat too much. Why do you think we might eat more food than we need to?

Name ______________________________

Read each of the stories carefully. Think about the **main idea** of each one. Circle the **best** answer.

1. There are green trees and orange trees. There are trees with flowers and trees with leaves. My favorite kind of tree is a Christmas tree.

a. Trees with light
b. Flowers in the garden
c. Different kinds of trees

2. I've got something in my hand. If you can guess what it is, I'll give it to you. It is long and yellow and grows on a tree. If you want to eat it, you will have to take off the outside. Do you know what it is?

a. Playing a guessing game b. Learning about trees c. Eating oranges

3. Yesterday I was so tired I started to yawn in class. Then Susie yawned, and Greg yawned, and Nancy yawned. Pretty soon, even the teacher was yawning. Everyone caught my yawn.

a. A yawn can be catching
b. Sleeping in class
c. My friend Nancy

4. We planted corn yesterday. It is my favorite vegetable. My mother makes corn muffins and corn cob pie. I could eat corn every day.

a. Popping corn b. The vegetable I like best c. Pie in the sky

Thinking Time

Read the next 2 questions carefully. Then answer them on the back of this paper.

5. Finish this story: "My favorite day is . . . Make the story tell something special about yourself.

6. In the third story, the girl yawned because she was tired. What could she do so that she wouldn't be so tired during the day?

© Frank Schaffer Publications, Inc.

Name ______________________________

Read the stories carefully. Think about the **main idea** of each one. Circle the **best** answer.

1. Look at this camel. Something is missing. Can you find what it is? Fill in the missing part with your pencil.

a. Painting pretty pictures
b. What camels carry
c. Finding something missing

2. A little dog is called a puppy. A tiny cat is called a kitten and a baby horse is a colt. Does anyone know what a little elephant is called?

a. Names for baby animals   b. Feeding the kitten   c. Gray elephants

3. People live in all different kinds of houses. They live in grass houses or ice houses or boat houses. I live in an apartment house. It goes up very high. I can see everyone's house from the top of my house.

a. How to build a house
b. Flying planes
c. Many different houses

4. I'm going to write a letter to my friend Tony. We moved away to a new city last summer. I will tell Tony all about our new house. I'll ask him to come and visit sometime.

a. Making the letter **B**   b. Writing to a friend   c. Paper kites

Thinking Time

Read the next 2 questions carefully. Then answer them on the back of this paper.

5. Moving to a new city can be fun, but it can be sad, too. What things would you miss the most if you had to move?

6. "My house is built on wheels. We can go on a trip to the mountains and take our house along with us." Draw a picture showing what you think this house looks like.

© Frank Schaffer Publications, Inc.

Name ______________________________

Read the stories very carefully. Think about the **main idea** of each one. Circle the **best** answer.

1. I have a big brother named Danny. I have a mother and father, too. Yesterday, my new baby sister came to live with us. Her name is Bonnie.

a. Big sisters b. Little things c. My family

2. Bees "buzz", cows "moo", pigs "oink", and birds "chirp". You don't always need to see an animal to tell what it is. Just close your eyes and listen very carefully.

a. Listening to animal sounds
b. A bird's nest
c. What eyes can see

3. What are hands for? Hands can wave "hello", turn pages in a book and pull a wagon. Hands can pet a kitten, let you stand upside down, and clap when you are happy. What would we do without hands?

a. Waving "hello" b. All the things hands can do c. Where books come from

4. I lost my first tooth today. His name is Bert. Bert and I have been together for seven years. Tonight I'll put Bert under my pillow and the fairy will take him away. I wonder if Bert will be someone else's tooth tomorrow?

a. Staying up late
b. What happens to a lost tooth
c. The good fairy

Thinking Time

Read the next 2 questions carefully. Then answer them on the back of this paper.

5. In the second story "close" your eyes means to "shut" them. If you say the "s" softly, "close" can mean something else. What is it?

6. "Everything has gone wrong today. I spilled my juice, lost my book, and shut the door on my finger. I'll be glad when today is over." What is the main idea of this story?

© Frank Schaffer Publications, Inc.

Name ____

Read the stories very carefully. Think about the **main idea** of each one. Circle the **best** answer.

1. Today is Tuesday. This is the best day of the week. My mother puts three chocolate chip cookies in my lunch—not just two. I wish every day were Tuesday.

a. Eating cookies and milk b. The best day of the week c. Why I like to eat

2. How many things do you know that are red? There is a sign that says "stop" and a valentine that says "I love you." There is an apple high in a tree and ice cream with a big cherry on top. And then there is me. I have hair that is as red as fire.

a. Stopping at a stop sign
b. Thinking about red things
c. Where to find snails

3. If I could have three wishes this is what they would be: (1) I would like a 15-speed bicycle that could fly. (2) I would wish for it to be summer all year long. (3) I would wish for three more wishes.

a. A bicycle for Christmas b. Wishes and more wishes c. A long hot summer

4. "Someone ate your pie, Dad, and I know who did it. A big green worm was hiding under the table. He must have been 20 feet long. When you went into the kitchen he stuck out his tongue and swallowed the pie all at once. Then he crawled out the window."

a. Worms in the kitchen
b. A pie-eating worm
c. A mad Dad

Thinking Time

Read the next 2 questions carefully. Then answer them on the back of this paper.

5. "John opened the closet door. He clapped his hands and smiled from ear to ear. His wish had come true." How did John feel? How can you tell how John feels if you can't hear him talking?

6. Read the fourth story again. Do you think a worm really ate the pie? Why not?

© Frank Schaffer Publications, Inc.

Name ____________________

Read the stories very carefully. Think about the **main idea** of each one. Circle the **best** answer.

1. When I grow up, I want to be a clown in the circus. I can go to many different places and stay up late at night. All my friends will come to see me.

a. Going to bed early b. Taking a trip c. What I want to be

2. If you want your wish to come true, you need to do three things: (1) Tie your feet together. (2) Jump backwards 12 times with your eyes closed. (3) Throw some water over your head. Be sure to do this outside so your mother won't get mad.

a. How to make wishes
b. Cooling off in summer
c. 12 things to do

3. Think of all the things your nose can do. It can smell a pie baking in the oven or a candle burning on a cake. A nose can hold glasses over your eyes so you can see. A nose can also give you a cold.

a. Blowing your nose b. Smelling apple pie c. The things a nose can do

4. Today I bought an orange lollipop. I licked it 56 times. There are still 12 more licks before I get to the stick. But I'm saving them for my dog Bemo.

a. A bone for Bemo
b. The licks on a lollipop
c. An orange stick

Thinking Time

Read the next 2 questions carefully. Then answer them on the back of this paper.

5. The boy in the first story wants to be a clown when he grows up. Would you like to be one too? Tell why or why not.

6. You shouldn't tell anyone what you're wishing for because then it might not come true. But you can draw a funny picture of your wish and let everyone try to guess.

© Frank Schaffer Publications, Inc.

Name ______________________________

Read the stories very carefully. Think about the **main idea** of each one. Circle the **best** answer.

1. Animals use their tails for many things. Cows shoo away the flies. A fish uses his tail to help him swim. The squirrel's tail is like a parachute when he jumps through the trees.

a. Animals that swim   b. How animals use their tails   c. Squirrels

2. Here is your pumpkin for Halloween. You can put him in the window tonight. But first he needs a face. On the back of this paper draw your own pumpkin. What kind of face will you give him?

a. Baking pumpkin pie
b. Dressing up for Halloween
c. Drawing a pumpkin face

3. Some animals have names to match the sounds they make. A mouse is called "Squeaky," and a duck is called "Quacker." The name I like best is "Hooty." Can you guess who it belongs to?

a. Animals that squeak   b. Names that go with animals   c. Milking a cow

4. Steve loves to tell riddles. Yesterday he told a very silly riddle in class, and this is what it was: "What happened when the boy dreamed he ate a five pound marshmallow?" Answer: "His pillow was gone!" Steve's riddles are very funny!

a. The disappearing marshmallow
b. A boy who likes to tell riddles
c. Eating in bed

Thinking Time

Read the next 2 questions carefully. Then answer them on the back of this paper.

5. Your eyes can see, your nose can smell, and your mouth can taste. A pumpkin's eyes, nose and mouth cannot do these things. Why?

6. You already know what a tail is, but what does "tale" mean? Use the word in a sentence.

Name ______________________________

Read the stories very carefully. Think about the **main idea** of each one. Circle the **best** answer.

1. How much wool does a lamb grow every year? About seven pounds altogether. That's enough to make two warm coats or four pairs of pants.

a. Making warm coats b. A seven pound lamb c. The wool from a lamb

2. DON'T eat with your fingers. DON'T drop your clothes on the floor. DON'T hit your sister. DON'T forget to take a bath. DON'T touch the pie. Does anyone have a DO that I can do?

a. Finding something to eat
b. Too many DON'T's
c. DON'T forget my party

3. In our town we have a very special store. Only children can go in. The store is so little that big people can't fit through the door. There are toys, games and books inside. It's so much fun. I'll be very sad when I grow up and have to stay outside.

a. Going to a circus b. A child's special store c. Feeling sad inside

4. "Uh-oh Billy, your mother is coming! She is going to be very mad if she finds a giraffe in your room. This is what we'll do. The giraffe can sit on the bed and then we can put the tent over his head. We'll tell your mom that we're going to camp in here tonight."

a. A camping trip
b. Helping mother
c. Hiding a giraffe

Thinking Time

Read the next 2 questions carefully. Then answer them on the back of this paper.

5. Finish this story: "I DON'T like to get up in the morning because . . . "

6. Hundreds of people live on an island. There isn't much land left. What kinds of buildings and houses would you build so more people could live on the island?

Name ______________________________

Read the stories very carefully. Think about the **main idea** of each one. Circle the **best** answer

1. I am going to sleep now. Please open the closet door and let all my dreams come out. This is what sleeping is for—dreaming.

a. Cleaning out the closet b. Why we go to sleep c. A bedtime story

2. Today I sat on my swing and watched the sun go down. First it went behind Mrs. Grundy's chimney. Then it passed the tallest tree in the park. It must be at Janey's house now. I can't see the sun, and I can't see Janey's house either.

a. Where Janey lives
b. Watching the sun set
c. Visiting Mrs. Grundy

3. Did you know that the peanut is not really a nut? It looks like one, but it's not. Peanuts are the seeds of a plant and belong to the pea family. Another name for a peanut is a "goober."

a. Peas in a pot b. A story about peanuts c. Planting seeds

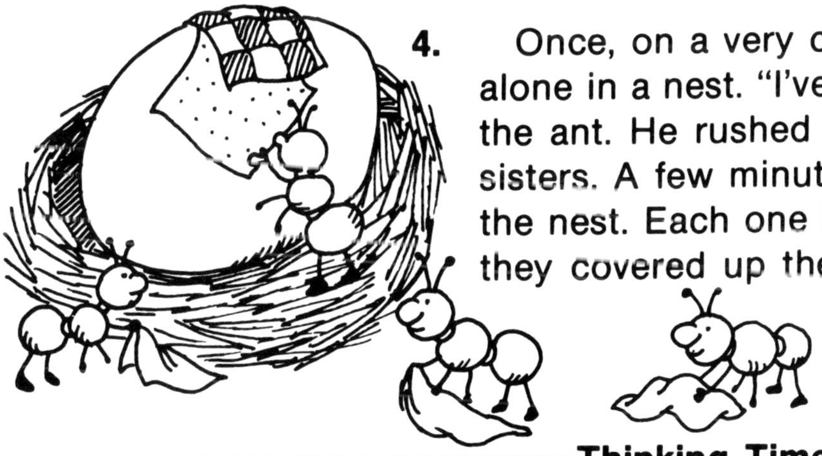

4. Once, on a very cold day, there was a little egg all alone in a nest. "I've got to keep this egg warm," said the ant. He rushed home and told his brothers and sisters. A few minutes later all the ants came back to the nest. Each one had brought his own blanket and they covered up the egg.

a. Eggs for breakfast
b. A lost bird
c. Warming up an egg

Thinking Time

Read the next 2 questions carefully. Then answer them on the back of this paper.

5. Peanuts come from seeds. If you went to the store and bought some flower seeds, what would you do so they would grow to be nice tall plants?

6. The first story says sleeping is for dreaming. What did you dream about last night?

Name ______________________________

Read the stories very carefully. Think about the **main idea** of each one. Circle the **best** answer.

1. What is strange about this story? "It was a very hot day in July. Debbie pulled her sled up the hill. She was wearing a bathing suit, mittens and a hat." Can you find the things that don't belong in this story?

a. Sliding on a sled b. Strange things in a story c. A strange looking boy

2. A ghost lives in my room, but only at night. He sits on my baseball bat at the bottom of my bed. His name is Jack. Someday I will go to his house in Lotta Land and show him how to play baseball.

a. Playing games
b. A friend named Jack
c. A bat called Jack

3. One day I was sitting on the grass all by myself. An ant came along and crawled up on my baby toe. He was carrying a piece of bread. It was so heavy, he had to lie down and rest on each toe. Finally the ant got so tired, he just ate the bread and walked away.

a. An ant who ate up a toe b. Running through the grass c. a tired little ant

4. There is a clock in my room. It hangs on the wall by my bed. This is a very different clock because it talks to me. Every morning the clock quietly says, "Tock, tick. Get up, Dick." If I don't wake up, it rings a very loud bell and yells, "Get out of bed!"

a. Singing clocks
b. Bells that yell
c. A talking clock

Thinking Time

Read the next 2 questions carefully. Then answer them on the back of this paper.

5. "Night" and "knight" sound exactly the same, but their meanings are different. Get out your dictionary. Look up "knight" and write the meaning of this word.

6. Just about everyone has a clock or a watch. Why is it important for us to know what time it is?

© Frank Schaffer Publications, Inc.

Name ______________________________

Read the stories very carefully. Think about the **main idea** of each one. Circle the **best** answer.

1. The very first bicycle had two wheels and a seat, but no handles or pedals. It was called a "hobby horse." It was hard work to push it along the ground with your feet.

a. Bicycle wheels b. A hobby horse that rocks c. How the first bicycle looked

2. Here comes that cloud again! Every time I go to the park to play ball that cloud comes around the corner looking just for me. Then it drops all its water just as I'm getting ready to bat the ball. Where can I hide from that cloud?

a. Watering the grass
b. A rain cloud that follows me
c. Clouds playing ball

3. "Everyone is coming out of the circus tent," Terry said. "I wonder if they liked the show?" Terry looked at everyone's face. One boy smiled and another boy laughed out loud. Terry could tell it was a good show. She didn't even have to ask. Faces tell a lot of things without saying a word.

a. What a face can say b. Watching the circus c. Making faces

4. I am going to be Little Bo Peep on Halloween night. My two little kittens are going to be my sheep. They will wear fuzzy sweaters, one orange and the other blue. Do you think it matters that they aren't white?

a. Little lost sheep
b. Making kittens look like sheep
c. Dressing kittens like Little Bo Peep

Thinking Time

Read the next 2 questions carefully. Then answer them on the back of this paper.

5. Draw a picture showing how this girl might feel: "Sara's little brother took her favorite book and left it out in the rain. All the words washed off the pages."

6. Guess who? He wears a heavy black coat and hat. He rides on a red truck and climbs up tall ladders. He can't do his job without using water.

Name ____

Read the stories very carefully. Think about the **main idea** of each one. Circle the **best** answer.

1. It's fun to make pictures from your fingerprints. I made a mouse out of one of my fingerprints. Can you make the other fingerprint look like a fish?

a. Fingerprint pictures
b. Drawing letters
c. A fishy story

2. "I look really beautiful," the rat said, combing her whiskers. "I took a bath this morning and scrubbed my ears and my back. I washed my hair and my toes too. Everyone should take a bath once a year like I do."

a. Brushing your teeth   b. The rat who took a bath   c. A year old rat

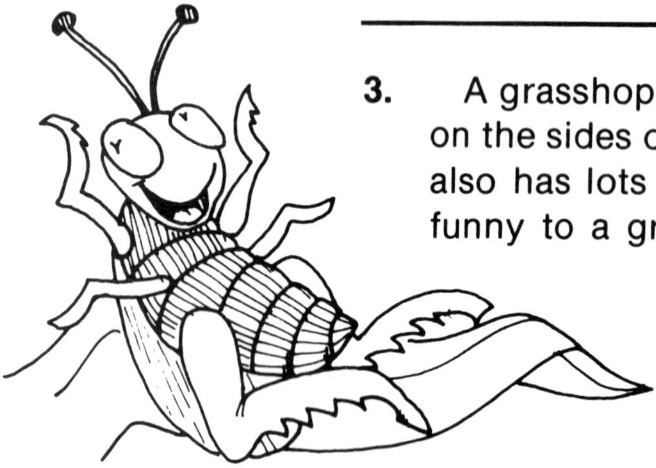

3. A grasshopper looks funny to me. It has two big eyes on the sides of its head and three more eyes on top. He also has lots of elbows and knees. I wonder if I look funny to a grasshopper?

a. Hopping in the grass
b. Smells in the air
c. What a grasshopper looks like

4. I have a dog named Sam. He is very lazy in the summer. It's much too hot for him to play. Sam sits under a tree all day and then goes into his doghouse at night. Sometimes he shoos away a fly with his tail, but that is just about all he does.

a. What Sam does in summer   b. Feeding a dog   c. Sleeping under the moon

Thinking Time

Read the next 2 questions carefully. Then answer them on the back of this paper.

5. If it were very hot one day, what are some of the things you would do to cool off?

6. Take a library book and turn to the first page of the story. After you read it, tell what the **main idea** of the story is.

© Frank Schaffer Publications, Inc.

Name ____

Read the stories very carefully. Think about the **main idea** of each one. Circle the **best** answer.

1. If you want to learn to do something well, you'll have to work hard and practice all the time. When Dorothy Hamill was learning to skate, she practiced seven hours a day and even longer on weekends.

a. Learning to skate
b. How to do something well
c. Working on weekends

2. The first time you hear your own voice on a tape you might be very surprised. You probably won't even know it's you! The sound you hear from your voice when you talk is different from the sound your friends hear.

a. Talking on a tape b. The sound of your voice c. Hearing friends talk

3. You probably never thought of this, but your thumb is a very handy thing to have. Try writing your name or tying your shoe without using your thumb. Can you zip a zipper without your thumb? Be nice to your thumb. It will do lots of things for you.

BE KIND
TO THUMBS WEEK

a. Why we need our thumbs
b. Learning to write your name
c. Zippers that have thumbs

4. Tomorrow is Turn-Around-Day at school. Everyone gets a turn to go to another class and teach something to the children. I'm going to the first grade and show them how to make ice cream. They will want me to be their teacher forever.

a. Turning around in circles b. Teacher for a day c. How to make ice cream

Thinking Time

Read the next 2 questions carefully. Then answer them on the back of this paper.

5. You have decided to paint a picture of the sun coming up. What things will you need to paint your picture? What time will you start painting?

6. John looked at the questions on the test and said, "Oh, no! I don't think I'm going to get a good grade on this test." Why do you think John felt this way?

© Frank Schaffer Publications, Inc.

Name ______________________________

Read the stories very carefully. Think about the **main idea** of each one. Circle the **best** answer.

1. Does your cat like to chew gum? My cat, Rufus, loves pink Snap-Happy Gum. His best trick is blowing a bubble that looks like an elephant!

a. Blowing up elephants
b. Teaching a cat a trick
c. A very silly cat

2. A very long time ago cave men used to live here. They didn't have any homework because they didn't go to school. The cave men played with dinosaurs and dragons, and they had lots of fun. I wish I could be a cave man.

a. Playing in caves b. A new pet c. Thinking about long ago

3. There is someone behind me that has been following me around all day long. He is much bigger than I am but I'm not afraid. When I eat he sits on the floor. When I go to bed he sleeps on the wall. He is my shadow. Look around—you might have one too.

a. Afraid of shadows
b. Someone who follows me
c. Sleeping on the floor

4. "I'd better not eat too many of these peas, Mom, or I might turn green. Then I won't be able to go to school. My teacher told be she doesn't allow green boys in her class. I'll eat three peas now and save all the rest until summer comes."

a. The boy who didn't like peas b. How peas grow c. Saving for summer

Thinking Time

Read the next 2 questions carefully. Then answer them on the back of this paper.

5. Years ago, when men lived in caves, they didn't go to school and they didn't go to the office. Name two things cave men might have done during the day.

6. Use all of these words and some of your own to write a silly sentence:
purple, hot dog, dinosaur, tail, burn

Name ______________________________

Read the stories very carefully. Think about the **main idea** of each one. Circle the **best** answer.

1. How many things can your tongue do? It can taste your food, lick your lips, say all your L's, and tickle the top of your mouth.

a. How a tongue tastes
b. Good things a tongue can do
c. Tasting food

2. "I have a very bad cold, Mom, and I think I'm getting the measles. I'm much too sick to go to school. I'd better stay in bed all day. What did you say, Mom? Today is Saturday? I'm feeling better already!"

a. Getting sick on Saturday b. A cold day c. Closing the schools

3. I have a big brown dog named Thumpy
He eats too much and looks a little Dumpy
One day, the cat scratched him and made him Grumpy
Now his head is very big and Lumpy

a. Making mother mad
b. A Grumpy, Lumpy dog
c. A big brown cat

4. There are some things that always come in pairs. We have two eyes, two ears, two hands and two feet. Do you think if we had two mouths we could talk to two people at the same time?

a. Hands that talk b. Things that come in pairs c. Drawing a face

Thinking Time

Read the next 2 questions carefully. Then answer them on the back of this paper.

5. Ted is going to get a job. He wants to save $30 before Christmas. Why do you think Ted wants to earn the money?

6. "Poor Nancy! This just isn't her day. This morning she burned her toast, lost her shoe and bumped her head." What would be a good title for this story?

© Frank Schaffer Publications, Inc.

Name ____

Read the stories very carefully. Think about the **main idea** of each one. Circle the **best** answer.

1. Hello! I'm a root. I belong to this tree right above my head. I have very long arms and legs. My job is to find water to feed this thirsty tree. Without me trees couldn't live.

a. Drinking a glass of water b. How roots grow c. What roots do

2. I have a pet I'll bet you have never seen before. It is a rabbikangacoon. It has the head of a rabbit, the body of a kangaroo, and the tail of a raccoon. There are only four left in the whole world. It sleeps upside down in a tree at night.

a. A strange looking pet
b. Four animals in a tree
c. Animals of the world

3. You bad old table! Did you see what it did to me, Dad? I was just sitting here eating my breakfast when the table grabbed my arm. It made me spill my milk. You better be nice to me, table, or I'll take you back to the store.

a. Eating breakfast b. Talking to a table c. Shopping for milk

4. Mom said she is going to "dress" our Thanksgiving turkey. I wonder what she is going to put on him, a coat and a hat? I guess she just wants him to look real nice when he comes to the table at dinnertime.

a. Putting a dress on a turkey
b. Setting the table
c. "Dressing" a Thanksgiving turkey

Thinking Time

Read the next 2 questions very carefully. Then answer them on the back of this paper.

5. A rabbikangacoon is a silly animal. Can you draw another funny-looking animal or person and give it a name?

6. All trees have roots. Something you have has roots too. What is it? (Ps-s-s-s-t, it's something on your head.)

Name ______________________________

Read the stories very carefully. Think about the **main idea** of each one. Circle the **best** answer.

1. "Fire" rhymes with "tire" and "smile" rhymes with "while." "Cattle" rhymes with "rattle" and "squirrel" rhymes with "twirl." I'll bet you can't think of a word that rhymes with orange, can you?

a. Twirling a squirrel b. Words that rhyme c. A rhyming song

2. The grass is black, the sky is red,
My cat has feathers, her name is Fred.
"Oink" says the cow, "Woof" says the bee,
I make things the way I want them to be.

a. A cat that barks
b. Painting farm animals
c. Doing things my way

3. Every day the sun comes up in the morning and goes down at night. The sun must get very tired of doing the same thing day after day. If I could be the sun just once, I would rise at night and go down in the morning. But then it wouldn't be daytime, would it?

a. The lazy old sun b. What I'd do if I were the sun c. Getting up in the morning

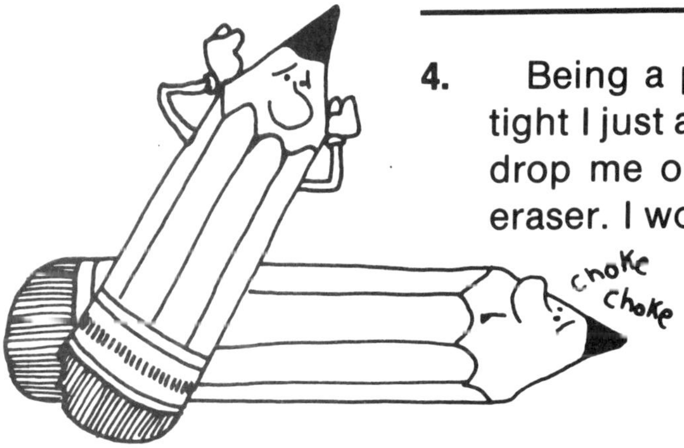

4. Being a pencil isn't much fun. Children hold me so tight I just about choke. They bang me on the table and drop me on the floor. Some children even eat my eraser. I would much rather be a pen living in a pocket.

a. A tight squeeze
b. Eating erasers
c. A pencil who wanted to be a pen

Thinking Time

Read the next 2 questions carefully. Then answer them on the back of this paper.

5. If you could change one thing to look just the way you wanted it to look, what would it be? Describe it in words or with a picture.

6. The first story is about rhyming words. Think of some words to rhyme with these words: bark, candy, lizard, price, skate, straw (Remember, only the endings have to rhyme.)

Name ______________________________

Read the stories very carefully. Think about the **main idea** of each one. Circle the **best** answer.

1. Find the ball to go with this sport: There are nine players on the team. The field is grass and shaped like a diamond. It is played in spring and summer.

a. Sports that have balls   b. Matching a ball to a sport   c. Summer games

2. Did you ever wonder what happened to Jake?
One day he woke up and had turned into a cake.
He only ate sweets and nothing more,
Now he's in a box on a shelf in a store.

a. What happens if you eat sweets
b. Where to buy a cake
c. Waking up a cake

3. I don't like Saturday. I never have. That's the day I have to clean up my room. I don't know why I have to put everything away. The very next day I take it all out again. When I grow up, I'm going to get rid of either closets or Saturdays.

a. How to get rid of Saturday   b. The day I don't like   c. Growing up in a closet

4. Have you ever seen a doodlebug? He is very little, round and gray. He lives in a hole close to a house. Get down on the ground, whistle near the hole, and call, "Doodlebug! Doodlebug!" He'll come up, but he won't be happy. You woke him up from his nap.

a. A round gray animal
b. Whistling a song
c. Digging holes near houses

Thinking Time

Read the next 2 questions carefully. Then answer them on the back of this paper.

5. The poem in the second story has a funny ending. You finish this poem:
I don't like carrots and I don't like peas
I always forget to cross my t's
But I do like chicken with lots of rice
____

6. What is the one thing you like to do the least? Why?

Name ____________________

Read the stories very carefully. Think about the **main idea** of each one. Circle the **best** answer.

1. Crickets don't make their chirping sounds with their voices. They just rub their wings together. It looks like they are playing the violin.

a. How crickets chirp b. Wings that won't fly c. A violin that chirps

2. The BooHoo is an animal that lives near the sea of VooLoo. He has 16 legs, 3 arms and a tail that looks like a fan. He likes hamburgers best of all. He told me so. Oh yes, the BooHoo can talk too!

a. A very funny animal
b. The sea of VooLoo
c. An animal that eats fans

3. How do you know fall is coming? I can tell because my mom takes my bathing suit and puts it in a box. Outside the air is getting colder and next week I go back to school. These are some of the signs of fall.

a. How to tell when it's fall b. Falling off a bike c. Packing up

4. Do you have some cream of giraffe soup here? My friend eats it all the time. That is how he got to be so tall. I need to get very big by next Thursday. Cowboy Joe is coming to town and he needs someone to rope horses for him. You need to be tall to do that.

a. Riding tall horses
b. Why I need to grow tall
c. Cooking cream of giraffe soup

Thinking Time

Read the next 2 questions carefully. Then answer them on the back of this paper.

5. The word "fan" has two different meanings. One is a thing; the other is a person. Look in your dictionary and write down what each one means.

6. Summer begins on June 21st. Write down some things that remind you of summer.

© Frank Schaffer Publications, Inc.

Name ____________________

Read the stories very carefully. Think about the **main idea** of each one. Circle the **best** answer.

1. Do you know what your name means? "Richard" means "brave" and "Dorothy" means "gift." Every name has its own special meaning.

a. A birthday gift   b. The meaning of names   c. Names for boys

2. My friend George told me a secret. He said not to tell anyone. I'm the best person to tell a secret to, because the very next day I can't remember the secret. A secret is safe with me.

a. The best secret keeper
b. Remembering late at night
c. Whispering secrets

3. When you sit down in a chair you can make your very own lap. Laps are good things to have. They catch crumbs that fall off the plate. You can put your tired hands to rest in your lap. Best of all, laps can hold a sleeping kitten.

a. Sitting down   b. The boy who didn't have a lap   c. Good things a lap can do

4. Dreams can take you places you have never been before. You can go by plane, on your bike, or even ride a cloud. Tonight let's go to the City of Ditty. Bring your banjo. The people play music there all night long.

a. Dreaming about planes
b. Moving far away
c. Taking a trip in a dream

Thinking Time

Read the next 2 questions carefully. Then answer them on the back of this paper.

5. "Plane" and "plain" sound the same but mean different things. Write a sentence for each word.

6. Names for holidays have special meanings. What do you think the name "Thanksgiving" means?

© Frank Schaffer Publications, Inc.

Answer Key

Name ______________________________

Write the numeral in the box that explains the sentence.

Who Said This?

1. Happy Birthday!
2. I'm high in the sky.
3. I'm so sleepy.
4. This tastes so good.
5. I love to read.
6. We won!
7. I like the rain.
8. Did you brush your teeth?

3
1
2
7
4
6
5
8

Page 1

Name ______________________________

Write the numeral under the picture that goes with the sentence.

What Tool Would You Use?

1. Please cut the bread, John.
2. A nail goes here, Sally.
3. This ice cream tastes yummy.
4. Cut this wood in half, please.
5. Can you hold the bolt tighter.?
6. This will help you push the needle, Sue.
7. Cut the paper in half.
8. Mom, the eye is too small.

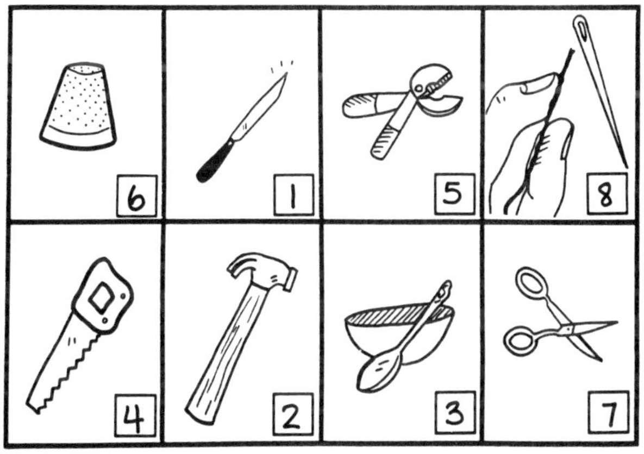
6
1
5
8
4
2
3
7

Page 2

Name ______________________________

Write the numeral in the box that explains the sentence.

All About Christmas!

1. He had a very shiny nose.
2. He brings presents.
3. The Christmas balls keep falling off.
4. No two are ever alike.
5. We need coal, a carrot, and a hat.
6. Hang it on the chimney.

3
6
1
Ho ho ho!
2
4
5

Page 3

Name ______________________________

Write the numeral in the box that explains the sentence.

What's the Weather?

1. Now we can ski.
2. Teddy needed an umbrella today.
3. It was hard to see across the street.
4. My kite flew as high as I could see.
5. We are ready for the beach.
6. I think it will rain today.

snow 1
sunny 5
rain 2
Yoo hoo! Where are you?
cloudy 6
windy 4
foggy 3

Page 4

Answer Key

Name ___________________________

Write the numeral in the box that tells how you can tell . . . .

Use Your Senses

1. The girl is singing.
2. The skunk is angry.
3. The food is good.
4. The trees are green.
5. The stove is hot.

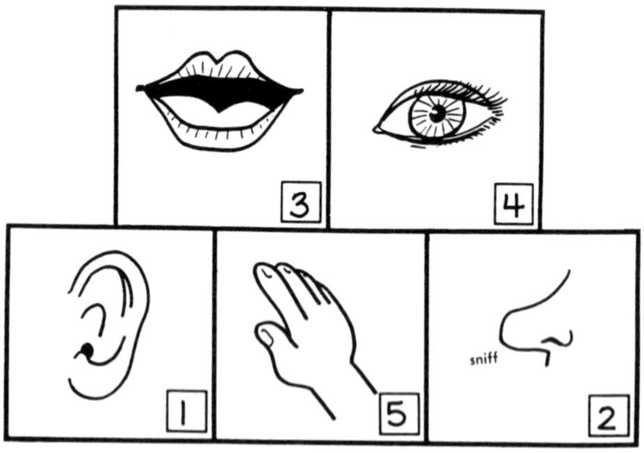
3
4
1
5
sniff
2

Page 5

Name ___________________________

Write the numeral in the box that goes with the sentence.

How Would You Feel?

1. You ran as fast as you could to school.
2. You went to bed too late.
3. Your best friend got the measles.
4. You got a new bike for your birthday.
5. The pieces didn't fit.
6. Your sister poked you.

grrr!
mad
6
sniff
sad
3
whew
hot and tired
1
huh?
puzzled
5
ho hum
sleepy
2
yipee
happy
4

Page 6

Name ___________________________

Write the numeral in the box that explains the sentence.

Where Will It Happen?

1. Jeff is going to go on a trip in the air.
2. Tom had his tonsils out.
3. My family is visiting the animals.
4. I have fun riding with my friends.
5. Janet is watching T. V.
6. We saw the clowns and tight-rope walkers.
7. Let's build a sand castle.
8. I'm getting a cool glass of milk.

zoo
3
airport
1
beach
7
hospital
2
circus
6
school
zoom
SCHOOL
4
home
5
refrigerator
8

Page 7

Name ___________________________

Write the numeral under the picture that explains the sentence.

How Would You Get There?

1. The children are ready to go to school.
2. My mother drove to work.
3. It's a long trip across the ocean.
4. My friend and I pedaled to the library.
5. We went straight up!
6. Dad paid the man for the ride.
7. We zoomed down the track.
8. We flew right over the clouds.

chug chug
7
BUS
1
8
S.S. LOUISE
3
5
2
4
TAXI
6

Page 8

Answer Key

Name ______________________

Write the numeral under the picture that explains the sentence.

Where Do They Live?

1. The bear slept all through the winter.
2. The puppy curled up and went to sleep.
3. The boy had some toys in his room.
4. She kept her eggs warm.
5. They swim in a school.
6. The hamster hid in the straw.
7. The chief wore green feathers.
8. Six dogs pulled their sled.

cave
1
nest
4
cage
6
doghouse
2
igloo
8
house
3
ocean
5
tepee
7

Page 9

Name ______________________

What Do You Need . . .?

zoom
4
tap
6
1
zip
5
swish
10

1. to write a newspaper story?
2. to take a picture of a baby?
3. to play in a band?
4. to be a pilot?
5. to be a baseball player?
6. to build a house?
7. to paint a picture?
8. to make clothes?
9. to fix the sink?
10. to sweep the floor?

click!
2
3
9
7
8

Page 10

Name ______________________

Write the numeral in the box that explains the sentence.

Who Said It?

1. The boys and girls left the room messy.
2. Someone dropped a spoon down the sink.
3. The food is sticking to the bottom of the pan.
4. The grass grew high after the rain.
5. That will be $5.82, please.
6. I'm going to listen to your heart beat.
7. I have very long hoses on my truck.
8. Please be very quiet.

plumber
2
gardener
4
fireman
7
doctor
6
clerk
ching
5
librarian
8
janitor
1
cook
3

Page 11

Name ______________________

Write the numeral under the picture that explains the sentence.

What Holiday Is It?

1. Santa Claus is coming to town.
2. John sent candy to his girlfriend.
3. Did you make a wish?
4. Today we give thanks.
5. That is a very scary mask.
6. How many eggs did you find?
7. The fireworks are beautiful.
8. Are you wearing green today?

Thanksgiving
4
Birthday
3
Easter
6
Christmas
1
July 4th
7
St. Patrick's Day
8
Valentine's Day
I Love You!
2
Halloween
5

Page 12

Answer Key

Name ______________________

Write the numeral in the box that explains the sentence.

Buzz — Bite — Bark — Meow!

1. Buzz - - - - - - - - - - - sting!
2. Ruff, ruff ruff!
3. Meow, meow — Meowwwwwwwwwww!
4. Gobble, gobble, gobble.
5. Peep, peep, peep.
6. Baa, Baa, Baa, Baa !
7. Oink, oink, oink.
8. Neigh, neigh, neigh, neigh!

7
3
5
8
1
4
2
6

Page 13

Name ______________________

Write the numeral under the picture that goes with the sentence.

What's the Sport?

1. Come on team, make a touchdown.
2. Hit the ball out of the park!
3. They were trying to hit the puck.
4. Dribble the ball down the court.
5. You can hit the ball with your head!
6. Grandad got a hole-in-one.
7. Your serve!
8. Aim for the head pin, Mark.

hockey 3
soccer 5
football 1
basketball 4
baseball 2
golf 6
bowling 8
tennis 7

Page 14

Name ______________________

Write the numeral under the picture that goes with the sentence.

What Would You Wear?

1. The waves are not very big.
2. Eric had crooked teeth.
3. Mother told me I could step in the puddles.
4. Don't crash!
5. I'm baking fudge brownies!
6. Don't freeze your fingers!
7. It was hard for me to see the blackboard.
8. Don't forget to wind it!

rain boots 3
mittens 6
watch 8
braces 2
apron 5
helmet 4
swim suit 1
glasses 7

Page 15

Name ______________________

Write the numeral under the picture that goes with the sentence.

What is the Food?

1. Pour me a tall glass, please.
2. Say, it slips off my fork!
3. All I need is jelly to make me happy.
4. We had a good Thanksgiving dinner.
5. I like this sandwich!
6. Fry it nice and crisp.
7. The rabbits ate all day long.
8. My teeth felt very cold.

bread 5
turkey 4
ice cream 8
milk 1
carrots 7
peanut butter 3
YUMMY BRAND
16 oz. size
spaghetti 2
bacon 6
munch

Page 16

© Frank Schaffer Publications, Inc.

Answer Key

Name ____________________

Write the numeral under the picture that goes with the sentence.

What Happened Before?

1. Mother answered the telephone.
2. It started to rain.
3. The flower grew.
4. Fred fell down. Ouch!
5. The boy went to bed.
6. The alarm clock went "buzz"!
7. We ate dinner.
8. The baseball went over the fence.

swish
z z z z z
4
5
6
3
ring!
POW
7
1
2
8

Page 17

Name ____________________

Write the numeral in the box that explains the sentence.

What Am I?

1. I am small, and I make honey.
2. I am large, and I swim in water.
3. I can fly and have webbed feet.
4. I go "cluck, cluck," and I give you eggs.
5. I have stripes and live in Africa.
6. I am furry and come from Australia.

6
1
2
5
3
4

Page 18

Name ____________________

Write the numeral in the box that tells about the thing that moves.

Moving Things

1. These go on the feet and have blades.
2. This is side-walk surfing with wheels.
3. I can ride the waves with this.
4. This has two wheels and a motor.
5. This has a powerful engine and goes into space.
6. This goes on tracks and pulls many cars.

U.S.A.
5
1
3
toot toot
chug
4
2
6

Page 19

Name ____________________

Write the numeral under the picture that explains the sentence.

What Time of Day is it?

1. I hear the lunch bell.
2. It's almost the next day.
3. Now I can see the stars.
4. The sun just went down.
5. Yum, we're having pancakes for breakfast.
6. The sun is coming up behind the hills.

night 3
noon 1
dawn 6
dusk 4
morning 5
bong
midnight 2

Page 20

© Frank Schaffer Publications, Inc.

Answer Key

Name ____________________

My Favorite Books

Lila loves to read. These are the books she likes best.

Black Beauty
Little Women
ALL ABOUT WILDFLOWERS
LAD A DOG
Georgie

fold -- fold

Put an X on Lila's favorite books.

Georgie
Insects in Your Yard
LASSIE Come Home!
LAD
Black Beauty
ALL ABOUT WILDFLOWERS
Little Women
My Friend Flicka

Number right ________

Number wrong ________

Brainwork! What are the names of your favorite books?

Page 21

Name ____________________

Mrs. Clark's Class

Super Job!! OUR BEST WORK
UNITED STATES
Today's Lesson:
DICTIONARY

fold -- fold

Put a box around everything that you saw in the classroom above.

Today's Lesson:
UNITED STATES
DICTIONARY

Number right ________

Number wrong ________

Brainwork! Which of the things on this page are in your classroom?

Page 22

Name ____________________

Foot Traffic

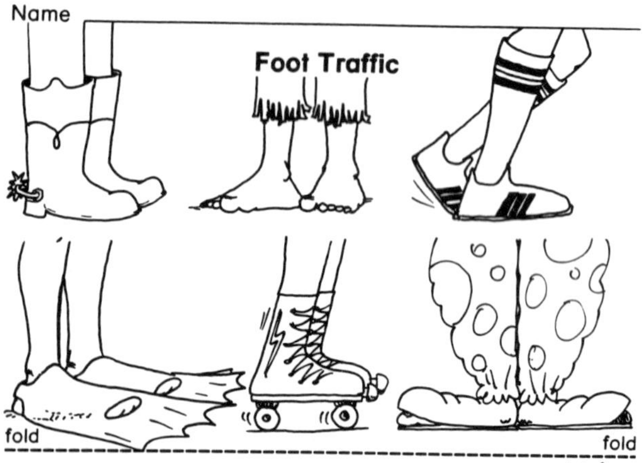

fold -- fold

Color the feet that are just like the ones above.

Number right ________

Number wrong ________

Brainwork! Draw your own feet!

Page 23

Name ____________________

Pete's Picnic

fold -- fold

How many of each of these were at Pete's picnic?

4
2
1
2
3
5

Number right ________

Number wrong ________

Brainwork! What are four of your favorite picnic foods?

Page 24

© Frank Schaffer Publications, Inc.

Answer Key

Name   Word configuration

Animal Word Shapes

In the story below, the names of animals are missing. Use the shape of the missing word to help you find the name in the Word Box. Write the words inside the shapes. Example: The monkey had a long tail.

Our class went to the zoo. We saw a tall giraffe munching on leaves. The hippos were taking a bath. Perched in a tree was a sleeping eagle. A lion roared in its den. A kangaroo hopped close behind its mother. The squirrel scurried up the side of a tree. Three snakes were coiled on a rock. Playful seals barked and dove for fish. The elephant searched for peanuts with its trunk. Six ducks floated on the pond. The big gorilla beat its chest. Many bats hung upside down in a dark room. As we walked by, a parrot said, "Hello." It was fun to see so many animals, but my favorite was the moose with the big antlers.

Word Box
squirrel
snakes
hippos
kangaroo
elephant
gorilla
lion
moose
giraffe
seals
ducks
eagle
bats
parrot

Try This! Neatly write the names of five animals in dark crayon. Leave space between them. Lay a fresh paper on top. Trace the shapes of the words. Cut the shapes out and scramble the pieces. Write each animal's name in its shape.

Page 25

Name   Animal names

Animals and Their Babies

The names of eight animals and their babies are hidden in this puzzle. First fill in the name of the missing animals or babies. Then circle each of the words in the puzzle. The animals are written across →, down ↓, and diagonally ↘.

kangaroo	joey	bear	cub
cat	kitten	duck	duckling
sheep	lamb	dog	puppy
horse	foal	cow	calf

Word Box
~~bear~~
~~calf~~
~~cat~~
~~cow~~
~~cub~~
~~dog~~
~~duck~~
~~duckling~~
~~foal~~
~~horse~~
~~joey~~
~~kangaroo~~
~~kitten~~
~~lamb~~
~~puppy~~
~~sheep~~

k	i	t	t	e	n	w	o	r	k
a	n	d	u	c	k	l	i	n	g
n	h	e	u	n	f	e	a	a	r
g	o	t	e	c	o	w	o	m	e
a	r	t	i	s	k	a	b	e	b
r	s	h	e	e	p	b	e	a	r
o	e	q	u	i	e	u	t	r	j
o	c	a	t	d	i	g	p	t	o
m	u	l	f	o	a	l	d	p	e
s	b	a	n	g	c	a	l	f	y

Try This! List eight more animals you know. Hide them in a word search puzzle. Switch with a friend and work each other's puzzle.

Page 26

Name   Skill: Classification

Go-Togethers

Look at each group of words below. First cross out the word that does not belong. Then add a word from the Word Box that does belong.

Word Box
refrigerator   sweater   fountain   towel   scissors   shovel

1. paper, pencil, eraser, stapler, ~~penguin~~, glue — scissors
2. toothbrush, ~~sausage~~, mirror, sink, soap, washcloth — towel
3. pans, stove, dishes, cupboard, ~~globe~~, toaster — refrigerator
4. shirts, ~~soil~~, skirts, shoes, pants, socks — sweater
5. ~~chocolate~~, hose, lawnmower, tools, paint, clippers — shovel
6. swings, benches, pond, flowers, grass, ~~pound~~ — fountain

Brainwork! For each list above complete this title: "Things You'd Find In..."

Page 27

Name   Skill: Context clues

What Does It Mean?

Choose a word from the Word Box to replace the boldfaced word in each sentence. Write it on the line. A dictionary can help you.

Word Box
shake brave smell copy little
strong tease choose disappear

1. The mouse felt **puny** standing next to the elephant. — little
2. Sour milk can have a bad **odor.** — smell
3. I get mad when big kids **taunt** my sister. — tease
4. The people will **elect** a new president. — choose
5. It was so cold I began to **quiver.** — shake
6. These trees look **sturdy** enough to climb. — strong
7. I saw the light in the distance **vanish.** — disappear
8. My brother can **imitate** the sound of a bird. — copy
9. The **courageous** knight fought the mean dragon. — brave

Brainwork! Choose two of the sentences above to illustrate.

Page 28

© Frank Schaffer Publications, Inc.

Answer Key

Name ______________________ Skill: Context clues

In Other Words

Choose a word from the Word Box to replace the boldfaced word in each sentence.

Word Box

trade	smile	hit	shine	path
spin	move	burn	extra	dressed

1. She can really **whack** the ball. hit
2. The dancer began to **twirl.** spin
3. I couldn't **budge** the heavy box. move
4. The teacher said to **exchange** papers. trade
5. The silly joke made him **grin.** smile
6. A hot iron can **scorch** clothes. burn
7. The **spare** tire is in the trunk. extra
8. We followed the **trail** back to camp. path
9. Waxing the car made it **gleam.** shine
10. The king was **clad** in royal robes. dressed

Brainwork! Write three sentences that might make a friend grin. Exchange papers and find out if they do!

Page 29

Name ______________________ Skill: Context clues

Learning to Skate

Read this story about learning to skate. Then answer the questions.

Many times I had **longed** to be able to ice skate. Finally my big sister agreed to teach me.

I was filled with **glee** as I laced up my skates for the first time. I thought I would be **gliding** over the ice in minutes. Was I surprised when I stood up and fell right on the ice. It sure was **chilly**!

My sister helped me up and said, "Don't **fret**. After a few more **tumbles** you'll be skating like a star!"

1. Which boldfaced word in the story means:

   a. cold? chilly
   b. wished? longed
   c. joy? glee
   d. worry? fret
   e. moving? gliding
   f. falls? tumbles

2. Circle the best answer.

   a. The word **chilly** has to do with
   food (temperature) skates
   b. Which would most likely fill you with **glee**?
   being sick (a surprise party)
   c. Which would you most likely **long** for?
   (a missing toy) a broken pencil
   d. When would you be most likely to **fret**?
   (if you missed the school bus) if you got a good grade

Brainwork! Draw and label five things that can glide through the air or on the water.

Page 30

Name ______________________ Logical thinking

What's the Question?

In each conversation below, the answer to a question is given but the question is missing! Choose and write the question from the Question Box that asks for the answer given. A sample is done for you.

What day is it?
It's Tuesday.

Question Box

What time is it?	How old are you?	How's the weather?
How much did it cost?	How are you?	What's for lunch?

1.  How much does it cost? — It was $1.95. 
2.  How's the weather? — It's warm and sunny. 
3.  What time is it? — It's 11:30 A.M. 
4.  What's for lunch? — We're having hot dogs. 
5.  How old are you? — I'm eight years old. 
6.  How are you? — I'm fine, thank you. 

Try This! Write the answers to three easy questions. Have a friend guess the questions.

Page 31

Name ______________________ Skill: Multiple meanings

Different Meanings

Look at the list below. Two different meanings are given for each word.

sign	1) a symbol	2) to write your name
dash	1) a small amount	2) to run quickly
chief	1) leader	2) first or main
trip	1) journey	2) to stumble
quarter	1) one-fourth	2) 25¢ coin
company	1) visitor or guests	2) business

Decide which meaning the boldfaced word has in each sentence below. Fill in (1) or (2). Then write the meaning on the line.

(1) ~~(2)~~ A. Be careful not to **trip** over the rock! to stumble

~~(1)~~ (2) B. We are having **company** tonight. visitor or guests

(1) ~~(2)~~ C. When it started to rain we made a **dash** for the house. to run quickly

~~(1)~~ (2) D. They turned left at the stop **sign.** a symbol

(1) ~~(2)~~ E. Mom gave me a **quarter** for my piggy bank. 25¢ coin

~~(1)~~ (2) F. The **chief** of police spoke to us about safety. leader

Brainwork! Write a new sentence for every boldfaced word. Have each sentence show the word's other meaning.

Page 32

Answer Key

Name ______________________ Skill: Multiple meanings

Which Scale?

Read these different meanings for the word **scale**.

1) thin plates on reptiles or fish.
2) an object used to measure weight
3) to climb up the side
4) a map marking for distance
5) a group of musical notes

1. Which meaning of **scale** (1, 2, 3, 4, or 5) does each picture show?

2. Choose the correct meaning of **scale** in each sentence. Write the meaning on the line below the sentence.

A. The **scale** shows that the town is 15 miles away.

a map marking for distance

B. Many dinosaurs had **scales**.

thin plates on reptiles or fish

C. I can play **scales** on the piano.

a group of musical notes

D. She put the meat on a **scale**.

an object used to measure weight

E. He **scaled** the high mountain.

to climb up the side

Brainwork! Look up the word **mark** in a dictionary. Write five of its meanings.

Page 33

Name ______________________ Identifying U.S. states

State Puzzle Poems

Do you know these states? Read the clues below. Write the name of the state on the line below its poem. Then write the state's two-letter abbreviation on its shape.

Florida (FL)
Alaska (AK)
Pennsylvania (PA)
California (CA)
Texas (TX)
Tennessee (TN)

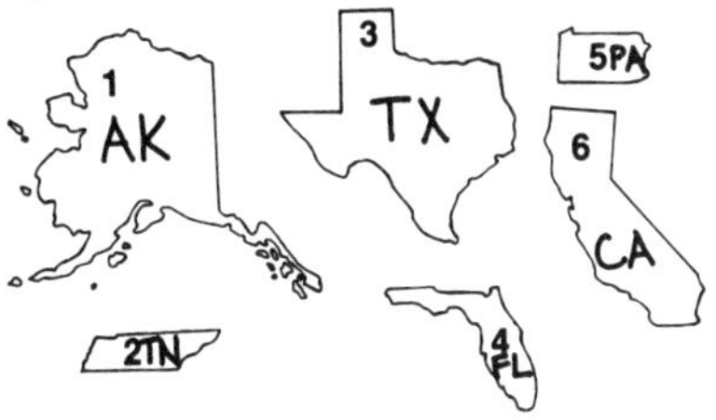

1. It's the largest state
and gets lots of snow.
You'll need a parka
to go there, you know.
Alaska

2. Nashville's the capital of
the Volunteer State.
And at its Ol' Opry
the music's just great!
Tenessee

3. Everything's big here
that we all know,
With Houston, Dallas,
and the famed Alamo.
Texas

4. Palm trees and oranges
and bright sunny beaches,
To the southernmost point
in the U.S. it reaches.
Florida

5. Named for William Penn
or so I've heard tell,
And here you can find
the Liberty Bell.
Pennsylvania

6. The Golden Gate bridge
and the tall redwood trees
Are two of its places
most likely to please.
California

Try This! Make up your own poem about another state. Trace its shape from a map. Then trade your state puzzle with a friend.

Page 34

Name ______________________ Skill: Social studies vocabulary, Context

Needs and Wants

Read this story about working together. The boldfaced words may be new to you. Their meanings are given below the story. Write the word that matches each meaning.

People everywhere have the same needs. They all need food, clothing, and shelter to **survive**, or stay alive.

In a community people **cooperate**, or work together, to get the things they need.

Some people provide **goods**, which are things made or grown for people to use. Other people provide **services**, or jobs that help others.

Besides needs, there are many things people want to make their lives more comfortable or fun. They buy many goods and services to enjoy in their **leisure**, or free time.

1. cooperate work together
2. leisure free time
3. survive stay alive
4. goods things made or grown for people to use
5. services jobs people do for each other

The pictures show jobs people do. Label them **goods** or **services**.

A.  services

B.  goods

Brainwork! Draw and label ten pictures of goods and services you use.

Page 35

Name ______________________ Skill: Science vocabulary, Context

Looking for Energy

Read this story about energy. The boldfaced words may be new to you. Their meanings are given below the story. Write the word that matches each meaning.

Scientists are looking for new **sources**, or places, to get energy. They are finding new ways to make, or **produce**, the power we will need in the future.

One kind of energy is **geothermal**. "Geo" means "earth" and "thermal" means "heat." Geothermal energy comes from heat that is already stored inside the earth.

Another kind of energy is **solar**. "Sol" means "sun." The sunlight is changed into energy we can use.

1. geothermal heat from the earth
2. solar from the sun
3. produce to make
4. sources places to get something

These pictures show kinds of energy. Label them **geothermal** or **solar**.

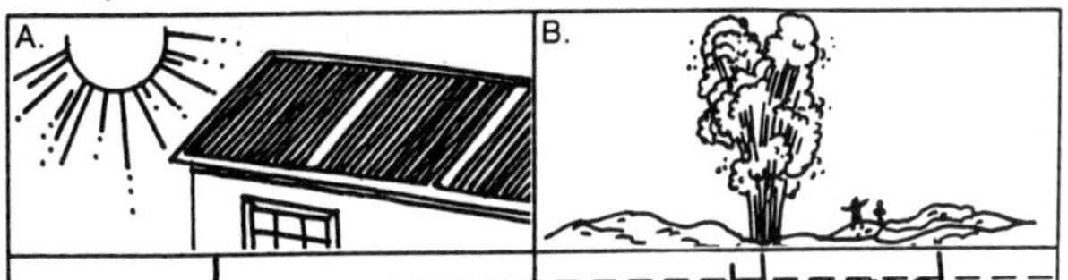

A. solar

B. geothermal

Brainwork! "-ology" means "the study of." Write what you think **geology** means. Then write the dictionary definition.

Page 36

Answer Key

Name — Syntax

That's Nonsense!

In each sentence below, the boldfaced word is not a real word. Even though the word is nonsense, you will be able to tell what it means from the way it's used. Choose a word from the Word Box to replace the nonsense word in each sentence. *a what ?*

Write the new sentences.

1. I had a **dringel** for lunch.
   I had a banana for lunch.
2. I read three **bleeks** last week.
   I read three books last week.
3. The **rawgis** took my temperature.
   The nurse took my temperature.
4. I wrote my name with a **jilcin**.
   I wrote my name with a pencil.
5. I'm **thaker** than my little brother.
   I'm taller than my little brother.
6. I enjoy **strobbing** in the pool.
   I enjoy swimming in the pool.
7. I brush my **seetles** every day.
   I brush my teeth every day.

Word Box
nurse
books
banana
taller
pencil
teeth
swimming

Draw a "dringel."	Draw a "rawgis."	Draw a "jilcin."
banana (drawn)	*nurse (drawn)*	*pencil (drawn)*

Try This! Invent your own nonsense words for: *school, bus, teacher, homework,* and *classroom.* Write a story that uses all of your invented words. Read it to a friend. Have him guess what your words stand for.

Page 37

Name — Communicating

Sign Language

People who cannot hear or speak are able to "talk" with their hands by using sign language. Many words and phrases have their own sign. All words can also be signed by finger-spelling using the **manual alphabet.**

Manual Alphabet

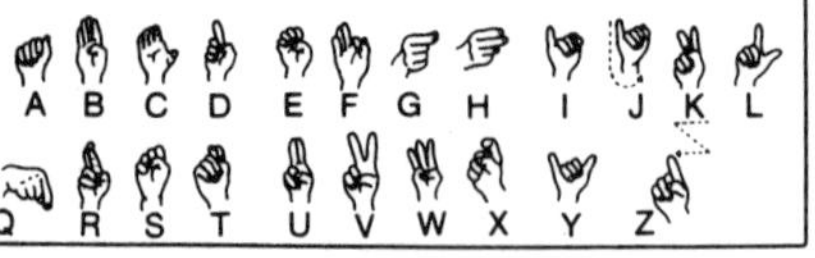

A B C D E F G H I J K L
M N O P Q R S T U V W X Y Z

Can you read these words? Write the letter below each sign.

S I G N I N G I S F U N

Practice signing the alphabet. Then sign the words and phrases below.

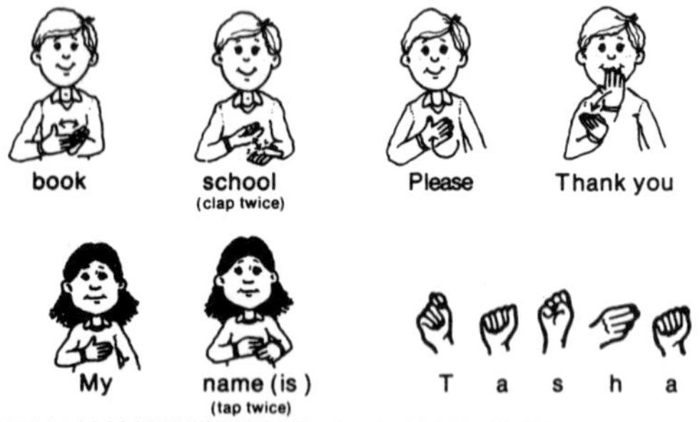

book
school (clap twice)
Please
Thank you
My
name (is) (tap twice)
T a s h a

Try This! Tasha has signed her name for a friend. Try spelling your name using sign language.

Page 38

Name — Using a code to solve riddles

Crack the Code

Use the code to write the correct letter below each symbol. You will discover the answers to some riddles. Draw a picture of each answer as you solve the riddle. (BEGIN).

HI

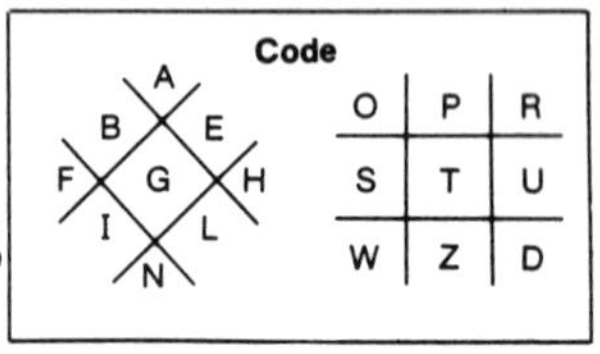

Code
A B E F G H I L N
O P R
S T U
W Z D

Example:
What do you always look toward but never see?
THE FUTURE

1. What gets wetter the more it dries?	2. What falls but never breaks?
TOWEL	RAIN
3. What has eyes but no face?	**4. What grows without getting any bigger?**
POTATO	FRIENDSHIP

Try This! Think of one of your favorite riddles. Write it and put the answer in code for a friend to solve.

Page 39

Name — Decoding, Handwriting

Rebus Fun

Letters, numbers, and pictures take the place of words in each sentence below. Use the Code Box to help you decode the sentences. Then write each sentence in your best handwriting.

Code Box

R are	leaves	handy	I
8 ate	can	my	bees
elbow	notebook	2 two	fancy
keep	B4 before	belt	skater
U you			

1. He B4 U.
   He leaves before you.
2. U have a .
   You have a fancy belt.
3. 2 stung .
   Two bees stung my elbow.
4. your .
   Keep your notebook handy.
5. 8 a of soup.
   I ate a can of soup.
6. R U a good ?
   Are you a good skater?

Try This! Write a message to a friend using some rebus words from the Code Box. Exchange papers to decode each other's message.

Page 40

Answer Key

Name ____________________ Skill: Decoding

Word Detective

Be a word detective. Use the clues in the Clue Box to help you decode the boldfaced words and answer the questions.

Clue Box

uni- one	**tri-** three
bi- two	**dec-** ten
cent- one hundred	

1. How many years in a **century**? one hundred
2. How many wheels on a **bicycle**? two
3. How many angles in a **triangle**? three
4. How many years in a **decade**? ten
5. How many legs on a **centipede**? one hundred
6. How many horns on a **unicorn**? one
7. How many years in a **centennial**? one hundred
8. How many wheels on a **unicycle**? one
9. How many legs on a **decapod**? ten
10. How many horns on a **triceratops**? three

Brainwork! Draw and label a unicycle, a bicycle, a tricycle. Write which you think would be the hardest to ride and why.

Page 41

Name ____________________ Compound words

Compound Confusion

The sentences below sound silly because one of the words that form the compound is incorrect. Choose a word from the Word Box to take the place of the boldfaced part of the word. Write the sentence correctly.

Word Box

drops rise run chalk works prints water shake suit

Example: The teacher wrote on the **checker**board.
The teacher wrote on the chalkboard.

1. We enjoyed fire**wood** on the Fourth of July.
We enjoyed fireworks on the Fourth of July.
2. The plane landed on the **door**way.
The plane landed on the runway.
3. Rain**coats** fell from the sky.
Raindrops fell from the sky.
4. My boots left foot**balls** in the snow.
My boots left footprints in the snow.
5. I put my clothes in the **book**case.
I put my clothes in the suitcase.
6. We woke up at sun**burn**.
We woke up at sunrise.
7. The fish swam under**ground**.
The fish swam underwater.
8. I greeted him with a hand**kerchief**.
I greeted him with a handshake.

Try This! Illustrate two pairs of sentences from above.

Page 42

Name ____________________ Compound words

Put It Together

Fix the mixed-up puzzle below. First cut the pieces apart. Then arrange the pieces so the words next to each other make the correct compound words. Glue the finished puzzle on another sheet.

side, door	walk, rail, bath	road, sail
bell, note, tooth	tub, book, birth, bed	boat, day, air
brush, after	room, noon, break	plane, fast

Try This! Make your own puzzle using rhyming words, opposites, or math facts.

Page 43

Name ____________________ Skill: Synonyms

Take My Place

Choose the word from the Word Box that could take the place of the boldfaced word in each sentence. Write it on the line.

Word Box

thick whole help choose careful piece

1. I will **select** a new tie for Dad.

choose

2. This box is heavy. Will you **assist** me?

help

3. Today we saw every animal in the **entire** zoo!

whole

4. I'd like a small **portion** of the cake, please.

piece

5. I didn't see you hiding in those **dense** bushes.

thick

6. Be **cautious** when crossing the street.

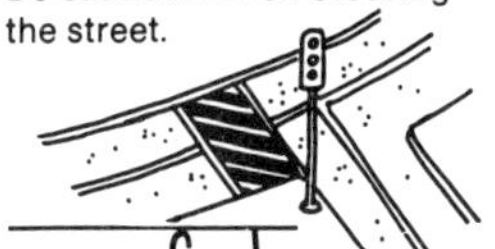

careful

Brainwork! Write five words that could take the place of the word *said*.

Page 44

© Frank Schaffer Publications, Inc.

Answer Key

Name ______________________ Skill: Synonyms

Figure It Out

Read each sentence. Use the picture clue to help you figure out the meaning of the boldfaced word. Circle the correct meaning. Write it on the line.

1. The workers are **constructing** a new house on our street.

building

building moving

4. The teacher corrected my spelling **error.**

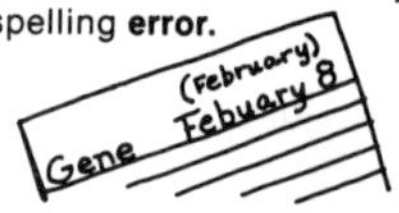

mistake

month mistake

2. Our plane **departed** at ten o'clock.

left

landed left

5. Blowing up a balloon **alters** its shape.

changes

changes colors

3. I waited for Sandy to **reply.**

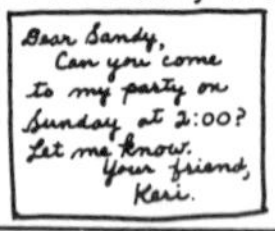

answer

answer visit

6. He will now **demonstrate** how the robot works.

show

believe show

Brainwork! List at least five things to which you could *reply.*

Page 45

Name ______________________ Skill: Antonyms

Get the Picture

Look at each picture and sentence. One word in the sentence is wrong. Circle the wrong word. Then write the word that would make the sentence true.

1. Pam is surprised because there is (something) in the box.

nothing

nothing everything

2. The plane will (leave) at one o'clock.

arrive

runway arrive

3. Tim doesn't know that there is a bee on the (front) of his shirt.

back

sleeve back

4. When you set the table, place the fork on the (right) side of the plate.

left

left same

5. Kim is (sad) because she found the missing bunny.

happy

tired happy

6. He stayed in bed because he was (well).

sick

sick young

Brainwork! The words *never* and *always* are opposites. Make a safety poster which has an "always" and a "never" rule.

Page 46

Name ______________________ Skill: Antonyms

I Meant to Say

Each sentence below was meant to say the opposite. Circle the incorrect word in each sentence. Choose a word from the Word Box to replace it. Rewrite the sentence using the new word.

Word Box					
sad	after	hard	odd	apart	borrow

1. I chipped a tooth on the (soft) candy.

I chipped a tooth on the hard candy.

2. Three and five are (even) numbers.

Three and five are odd numbers.

3. My puzzle pieces fell (together).

My puzzle pieces fell apart.

4. June comes (before) May.

June comes after May.

5. I was (happy) when my friend moved.

I was sad when my friend moved.

6. May I (lend) your eraser?

May I borrow your eraser?

Brainwork! Write each of these words and its opposite: first, began, mean, give, same, young, noise, and always.

Page 47

Name ______________________ Synonyms and antonyms

M_ssing Lett_rs

Dr. Find-it, the word detective, is faced with a puzzling case. It seems that letters are missing from all kinds of words. Her only clue is that the second word in each pair is a synonym or antonym of the first. She's stumped by the case because she has forgotten that a synonym is a word that means almost the same as another word, and an antonym means the opposite. Help Dr. Find-it solve the case by filling in the missing letters.

	Synonym		Antonym
1. cap	hat	16. near	far
2. little	small	17. above	below
3. store	shop	18. white	black
4. grin	smile	19. buy	sell
5. shove	push	20. wise	foolish
6. begin	start	21. soft	hard
7. ill	sick	22. huge	tiny
8. scream	yell	23. friend	enemy
9. fix	repair	24. truth	lie
10. gift	present	25. cool	warm
11. happy	glad	26. early	late
12. aid	help	27. quiet	loud
13. error	mistake	28. loose	tight
14. weep	cry	29. asleep	awake
15. halt	stop	30. close	open

Try This! Use graph paper to make a word search of synonyms or antonyms.

Page 48

© Frank Schaffer Publications, Inc.

Answer Key

Name ______________________ Skill: Homonyms

Which One?

Look at each pair of words in the Word Box. Read the clues carefully to find which word belongs in the puzzle.

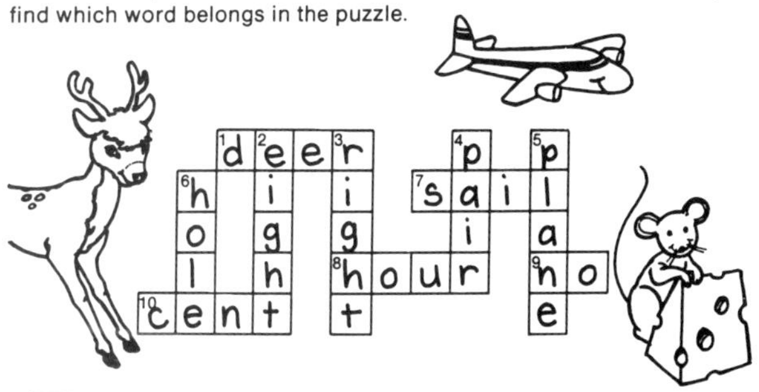

1 deer
2 eight
3 right
4 pair
5 plane
6 hole
7 sail
8 hour
9 no
10 cent

Word Box

sale-sail	whole-hole	sent-cent	pair-pear	our-hour
dear-deer	plane-plain	no-know	write-right	ate-eight

Across
1. an animal with antlers
7. to travel across water
8. 60 minutes of time
9. the opposite of yes
10. a penny

Down
2. the number before nine
3. the opposite of wrong
4. a set of two
5. a flying machine
6. an opening

Brainwork! Write a sentence to show the meaning of the unused word in each pair.

Page 49

Name ______________________ Skill: Homonyms

The Right Words

Some words sound alike but have different spellings and meanings. Look at the pairs of words in the Word Box. Read the story below. Look for the incorrect words and circle them. Then rewrite the story using the right words.

Word Box

road	waist	lone	weight	by
rode	waste	loan	wait	buy

Land of His Own

The cowboy (road) his horse into town. He didn't (waist) any time getting there. He went to the bank to get a (lone). He had to (weight) awhile. But soon he had money to (by) land of his own!

BANK
GENERAL STORE

Land of His Own

The cowboy rode his horse into town. He didn't waste any time getting there. He went to the bank to get a loan. He had to wait awhile. But soon he had money to buy land of his own!

Brainwork! Write a story using one word from each pair of words in the Word Box. Be sure to use the word with the right meaning.

Page 50

Name ______________________ Graphic expressions

I See What You Mean

wiggle broken

When you read the words *wiggle* or *broken* above, you can almost see their meanings. You can show the meanings of some words by the way you write the letters.

Read each word below. Use special letters to write the word in a way that shows its meaning.

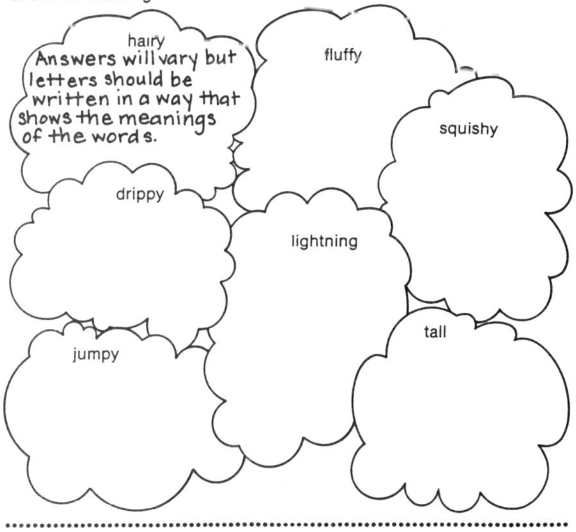

hairy
Answers will vary but letters should be written in a way that shows the meanings of the words.
fluffy
squishy
drippy
lightning
jumpy
tall

Try This! Write three sentences in which at least one of the words is written in a way that shows its meaning. Example: I saw a FAT worm.

Page 51

Name ______________________ Skill: Pronoun referents

Good Sports

Bill and Sara are brother and sister. They are on the same soccer team. Sara is an excellent kicker. **She**[1] scores many goals. Bill is a terrific goalie. Many times **he**[2] keeps the other team from scoring. Bill and Sara often hear their parents cheering **them**[3] on. They say **it**[4] helps them play their best. They don't always win the game, but **both**[5] always enjoy **it**.[6]

Each numbered word in the story stands for the name of someone or something in the story. Decide what each word replaces. Write your answers on the lines below.

1. She— Sara (Bill / Sara)
2. He— Bill (Bill / Sara)
3. them— Bill and Sara (Bill and Sara / Bill and Sara's parents)
4. it— cheering (scoring / cheering)
5. both— Bill and Sara (Bill and Sara / Bill and Sara's parents)
6. it— the game (winning / the game)

Brainwork! What sport do you enjoy playing or watching? Write about it.

Page 52

© Frank Schaffer Publications, Inc.

Answer Key

Name______ Skill: Word patterns—final e

Pattern Pairs

Write the correct word from each pair to complete each sentence.

1. There is a pine tree in the yard. — pin
2. You can hold cloth together with a pin. — pine
3. I need a scrap of cloth. — scrap
4. I got a scrape when I fell. — scrape
5. The cute puppy wanted to play. — cut
6. I cut the paper in half. — cute
7. The bird likes to tap on the window. — tap
8. Use tape to hold up the sign. — tape
9. The apple was ripe. — rip
10. I got a rip in my new jacket. — ripe
11. We plan to take a trip there. — plan
12. Grandpa came on a plane. — plane

Brainwork! Choose a pair of sentences above to copy and illustrate.

Page 53

Name ______ Double letters

Seeing Double

The words in each list contain double letters. Use the clues to complete the words.
Write the missing letters on the blanks.

full — filled up
dull — not sharp
jelly — sweet bread spread
dollar — type of money
collar — on your shirt
valley — between mountains
million — a large number
shells — found on a beach
balloon — filled with air

tooth — in your mouth
moon — seen at night
school — a place to learn
loose — not tight
hoof — a horse's foot
choose — make a choice
spool — holds thread
smooth — not rough
food — what we eat

green — a color
three — after two
queen — king's wife
sheet — put on a bed
breeze — a soft wind
deep — not shallow
knees — where legs bend
squeeze — hold tightly

Try This! Pick a pair of double letters such as *rr*, *ss*, *dd*, or *tt*. Make a "Seeing Double" puzzle for a friend to solve.

Page 54

Name ______ Categorizing

Getting In Shape

Write each word from the Word List in the shape where it belongs.

Word List
train
Jefferson
coat
New York
pine
Reagan
bus
oak
Texas
dress
ship
shirt
plane
California
Lincoln
apple
palm
pants
Kennedy
Florida

Clothing: coat, dress, shirt, pants

Trees: pine, oak, apple, palm

Presidents: Jefferson, Reagan, Lincoln, Kennedy

States: New York, Texas, California, Florida

Transportation: train, ship, bus, plane

Try This! Draw another category shape. Write five words inside.

Page 55

Name ______ Vocabulary

Start With a Vowel

Begin with a vowel and add a letter to each line to make a new word. The new letter may be added to the beginning, middle, or end of the word above it. There is a clue beside the new word to help you.

1) a
pa (dad)
pal (friend)
pail (bucket)

2) e
me (myself)
men (opposite of women)
mean (cruel)

3) i
hi (hello)
hip (part of body above the leg)
ship (boat)

4) o
no (opposite of yes)
now (present time)
snow (flakes of ice)

5) u
up (opposite of down)
pup (young dog)
pump (machine that supplies gasoline)

6) y
my (belongs to me)
May (name of a month)
many (a lot)

Try This! Make your own word puzzle. Share it with a friend.

Page 56

Answer Key

Name — Vocabulary

Word Towers

Each word tower in this castle is made by adding one letter to the beginning or end of a word to make the next word. Use the clues to help you complete each word tower. Write one letter in each blank.

Example:
- in — not out
- pin — used to fasten
- spin — turn around

1.
- ate — had eaten
- late — not early
- plate — used to serve food

2.
- rain — falling water
- train — runs on tracks
- strain — filter

3.
- myself — me
- grown boys — men
- fix — mend

4.
- think ahead — plan
- aircraft — plane
- heavenly body — planet

Try This! Build your own word tower with clues for a friend to solve.

Page 57

Name — Counting syllables

Picture Perfect

Color the design below by following these directions.

Color one-syllable words blue.

Color two-syllable words green.

Color three-syllable words yellow.

lake · tur tle · ba nan a

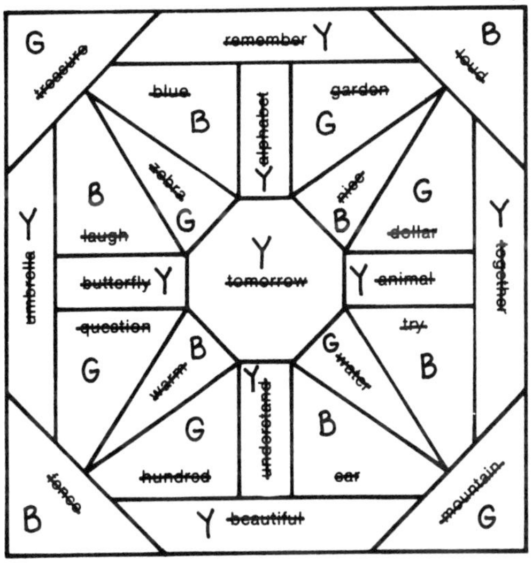

Try This! Draw your own design. Make a new puzzle for a friend to color.

Page 58

Name — Word discrimination

Forward and Backward

To solve each puzzle below, use the clues to discover a special pair of words. The second word is the first word *backwards!*

- a number word — ten; used to catch fish — net
1. used for frying — pan; a short sleep — nap
2. right away — now; finished first in a race — won
3. not all — part; catch and hold — trap
4. animals to keep — pets; put your foot on — step
5. friend — pal; appears when you sit — lap
6. swallow hard — gulp; at the end of a wire — plug
7. shines at night — star; small furry animals — rats
8. crunchy to eat — nuts; sudden shock — stun

Try This! Some words are spelled the same forward and backward like the word *dad*. Think of three or more words like this. Write them.

Page 59

Name ______ Skill: Commonly misused words

Which Is It?

Look at each pair of words below. They look almost the same but they have different meanings. Choose the correct word for each sentence. Fill in the ○ above the word.

metal—shiny, hard material; **medal**—an award	**through**—in one side and out the other; **thorough**—complete	**then**—at that time; **than**—a comparison

1. Mom told me to do a ____ job of cleaning my room. ○ through ● thorough
2. The dog barked, ____ he wagged his tail. ● then ○ than
3. I got a ____ for first place in the contest. ● medal ○ metal
4. The railroad track went ____ a long tunnel. ● through ○ thorough
5. My new bike is bigger ____ my old one. ○ then ● than
6. The tent was made of cloth with ____ poles. ○ medal ● metal

Brainwork! Use each pair of words in a sentence. Example: I used to be shorter **than** my sister, but **then** I grew!

Page 60

© Frank Schaffer Publications, Inc.

Answer Key

Name ______ Skill: Commonly misused words

Not Quite

Some words look very much alike but have different meanings. Look at the words and their meanings below. Then choose the correct word for each sentence. Fill in the ◯ above the word and write it on the line.

quite—very **quiet**—not noisy	**loose**—not tight **lose**—misplace	**guest**—visitor **guessed**—made a guess

1. We had a guest for dinner. ● guest ◯ guessed
2. I promise not to lose the note. ◯ loose ● lose
3. The children kept quiet during the fire drill. ◯ quite ● quiet
4. The weather was quite hot yesterday. ● quite ◯ quiet
5. The children guessed who was behind the mask. ◯ guest ● guessed
6. My tooth was loose so I didn't want to eat an apple. ◯ lose ● loose

Brainwork! "I **guessed** we were having a **guest**." Write sentences using the other two pairs of words from the Word Box.

Page 61

Name ______ Skill: Commonly misused words

A Close Call

Look at the words and meanings below. Choose the correct word to complete each sentence. Then write the meaning of the word you chose on the line below the sentence.

desert—very dry land
dessert—after-meal treat

1. Dad made us pudding for a special dessert.
   after meal treat
2. We drove across miles of sandy desert.
   very dry land

lose—misplace
loose—not tight

3. My brother's sweater was too loose.
   not tight
4. The money is in my pocket so I won't lose it.
   misplace

single—only, one
signal—warning sign

5. The single letter in the mailbox was for me.
   only, one
6. The red light was a signal to stop.
   warning sign

Brainwork! What can't you do with a door? Clothes it! Write two riddles like this using the words **picture** and **pitcher.**

Page 62

Name ______ Following directions

Secret Color Code

Reading and writing coded messages is fun. To read or decode this message, circle the words that come after colors. Then write the circled words on the line below the message.

My yellow (Meet) work red (me) elephant pink (in) the seven hamburger blue (the) school purple (park) cow.

Meet me in the park.

Use these three easy steps to write or encode a message.

1. Write the message leaving large spaces between the words.
   Example: I like you
2. Write a color before each of the words in the message.
   Example: orange I green like brown you
3. Fill in the rest of the blank spaces with other words.
   Example: Can orange I bicycle the green like shoes desk work secret flowers brown you zoo television bus now.

Write your own message using the secret color code.

Secret messages will vary.

Try This! Switch with a friend and decode each other's message.

Page 63

Name ______

Directions:

- ☑ Draw a line to match each picture and word.
- ☑ Underline the vowel in each word.
- ☑ Circle the two words that rhyme.
- ☑ Make a box around the longest word.

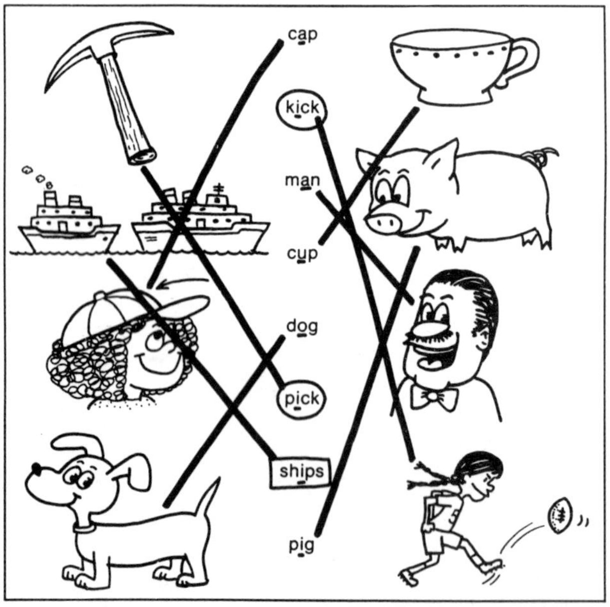

cap
kick
man
cup
dog
pick
ships
pig

Page 64

Answer Key

Name ______________________________

Directions:
☑ Match the words in the box to make a new word.
☑ Write the new words.
☑ Draw a picture for each word.
☑ Number the words in abc order (write the number in the ○).

base	news	flash	tooth	sun
paper	brush	ball	flower	light

Words	Pictures
① baseball	picture of baseball
③ newspaper	picture of newspaper
② flashlight	picture of flashlight
⑤ toothbrush	picture of toothbrush
④ sunflower	picture of sunflower

Page 65

Name ______________________________

Directions: In each row:
☑ Circle words with the same vowel sound.
☑ Underline the word that rhymes with the first word.
☑ Find a rhyming word that fits into each word shape below.
☑ Write the rhyming words in the correct shape.

1. cat	rat	sand	rip	and
2. red	leg	bed	egg	saw
3. fun	fan	sun	hut	lift
4. lip	kite	wig	fin	drip
5. hot	rod	slot	on	hope

rat bed sun

drip slot

Page 66

Name ______________________________

Directions:
☑ Write a word in each shape. Check off the words as you use them.
☑ Read the sentences.
☑ Write the number of the missing word.

Words to use
1. write
2. friend
3. basket
4. bicycle
5. under
6. ready

bicycle
under
ready write
friend
basket

Sentences
Kim is my best 2 .
I found the book 5 my bed.
Are you 6 to start?
Put the apples in the 3 .
Did you ride your 4 today?
1 your name on your paper.

Page 67

Name ______________________________

Directions:
☑ Fill in the missing letters on the chart.

*	A	B	C	*
D	E	F	G	H
I	J	K	L	M
N	O	P	Q	R
S	T	U	V	W
*	X	Y	Z	*

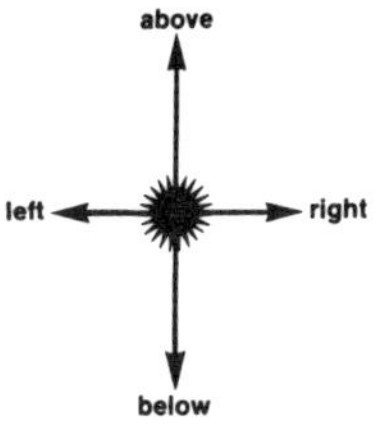

G I R A F F E
1 2 3 4 5 6 7

☑ On ___ 1 write the seventh letter of the alphabet.
☑ On ___ 6 write the letter before G.
☑ On ___ 3 write the letter to the right of Q.
☑ On ___ 2 write the letter below D on the chart.
☑ On ___ 7 write the letter to the right of D.
☑ On ___ 5 write the letter to the left of G.
☑ On ___ 4 write the letter above E.

Page 68

© Frank Schaffer Publications, Inc.

Answer Key

Name ______________________________

Directions:

☑ Fill in the missing numbers on the number chart.
☑ Write the numbers 1 to 12 on clock #1.
☑ Write the numbers I to XII (Roman Numerals) on clock #2.
☑ Draw an hour hand on clock #1. Make the clock say 5 o'clock.
☑ Draw an hour hand on clock #2. Make the clock say 8 o'clock.

Number Chart

1	2	3	4	5	6	7	8	9	10	11	12
I	II	III	IV	V	VI	VII	VIII	IX	X	XI	XII

Clock #1

Clock #2

Page 69

Name ______________________________

Directions:

☑ Use a letter from the box to complete each word.
☑ Cross out the letter that you used.
☑ On the ___ write a word with the three letters you have left.
☑ In the ☐ draw a picture to go with the word.

b_i_ke
shi_p_
ro_s_e
co_n_e
ska_t_e
s_o_ck
b_u_s
_b_ook
_c_ake
_s_ _u_ _n_

picture of sun

~~t~~	~~i~~
~~u~~	~~b~~
~~n~~	~~o~~
~~p~~	~~s~~
n	~~c~~
u	s

Page 70

Name ______________________________

Directions:

☑ Use the chart to fill in dates on the calendar.
☑ Fill in all the missing numbers up to 31.

Row	Day	Date
X	Tuesday	18
●	Saturday	15
▲	Saturday	1
◆	Thursday	6
▌	Friday	28
+	Sunday	30
◆	Monday	3
X	Wednesday	19

	Sunday	Monday	Tuesday	Wednesday	Thursday	Friday	Saturday
▲							1
◆	2	3	4	5	6	7	8
●	9	10	11	12	13	14	15
x	16	17	18	19	20	21	22
▌	23	24	25	26	27	28	29
+	30	31					

Page 71

Name ______________________________

Directions:

☑ Mark the ○ to show the answers in box #1
☑ In box #2 mark ☺ if word is spelled correctly, ☹ if word is spelled wrong.

#1

6+2	6 ○	8 ●	4 ○
7+1	8 ●	7 ○	9 ○
4-0	0 ○	4 ●	1 ○
5-3	8 ○	6 ○	2 ●
2+2	4 ●	2 ○	1 ○
6+0	0 ○	6 ●	5 ○
4+1	5 ●	6 ○	3 ○
7-2	3 ○	5 ●	7 ○

#2

Word	☺	☹	Word	☺	☹
pig	●	○	bed	●	○
tup	○	●	dosh	○	●
fish	●	○	dob	○	●

Page 72

© Frank Schaffer Publications, Inc.

Answer Key

Name ______________________________

Directions:
- ☑ Color one big ○ red.
- ☑ Color one big ○ blue.
- ☑ Color one big ○ yellow.

} Placement of answers may vary.

- ☑ With purple, color the small circle between red and blue.
- ☑ With green, color the small circle between blue and yellow.
- ☑ With orange, color the small circle between yellow and red.
- ☑ Fill in the **Color Chart** to show how to make colors. Choose two to make each color.

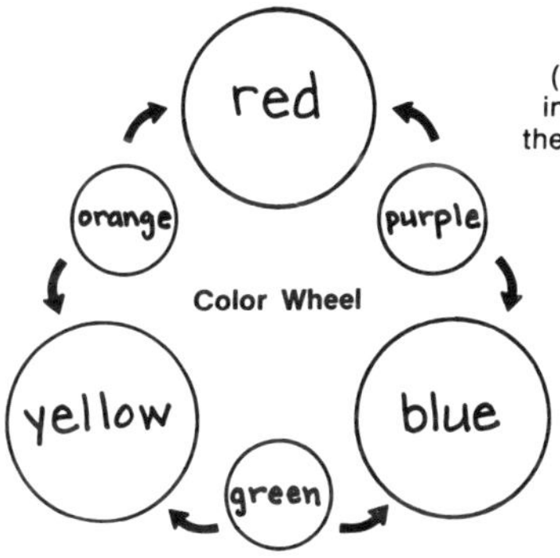
red
orange
purple
Color Wheel
yellow
blue
green

(To make the colors in the small ○ use the color on each side.)

Color Chart

To Make	Mix Red	Mix Blue	Mix Yellow
Orange	●	○	●
Green	○	●	●
Purple	●	●	○

Page 73

Name ______________________________

Directions: Use the words in the box.
- ☑ Circle the number words.
- ☑ Draw a line under the color words.
- ☑ Put a box around the animal words.
- ☑ Draw a line through all other words.
- ☑ Count and fill in the chart.

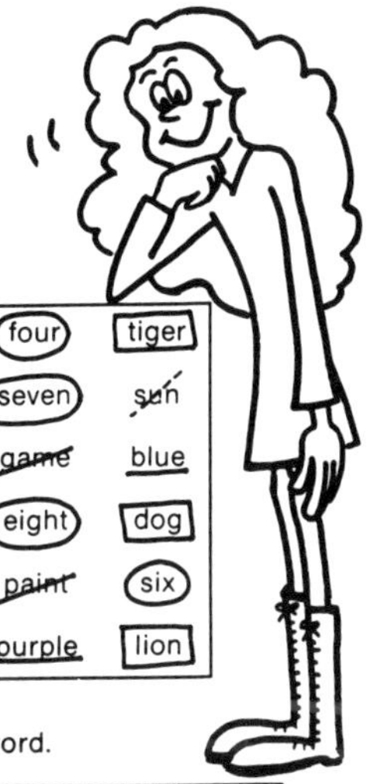

(one)	[cat]	black	(four)	[tiger]
red	[mouse]	(zero)	(seven)	~~sun~~
(ten)	~~lunch~~	(two)	~~game~~	blue
white	~~hat~~	[rat]	(eight)	[dog]
[horse]	~~teacher~~	yellow	~~paint~~	(six)
green	(three)	~~funny~~	purple	[lion]

Chart—Color one □ for each word.

Kinds of words	How many?	Total
Number words		9
Color words		7
Animal words		7
Other words		7

Arf.

Page 74

Name ______________________________

Directions:
- ☑ Draw a line under the numbers you use to count by fives.
- ☑ Circle the numbers you use to count by tens.
- ☑ Draw a box around the number that is the same as your age. (answer will vary)

1	2	3	4	5	6	7	8	9	10	11	12
13	14	15	16	17	18	19	20	21	22	23	24
25	26	27	28	29	30	31	32	33	34	35	36
37	38	39	40	41	42	43	44	45	46	47	48
49	50	51	52	53	54	55	56	57	58	59	60
61	62	63	64	65	66	67	68	69	70	71	72
73	74	75	76	77	78	79	80	81	82	83	84
85	86	87	88	89	90	91	92	93	94	95	96
97	98	99	100								

Page 75

Name ______________________________

Directions:
- ☑ Write words from the box on the chart.
- ☑ Check off the words as you write them.
- ☑ Count the words in each list. Write the number in the last box in each row.
- ☑ Answer the questions below the chart.

✓bike	✓game	✓coat	✓cards	✓apple
✓hat	✓meat	✓car	✓shirt	✓bus
✓cookie	✓shoes	✓ball	✓cheese	✓socks
✓jeans	✓train	✓bread	✓jet	

	To Eat	To Wear	To Play	To Ride
	apple	coat	game	bike
	meat	hat	cards	car
	cookie	shirt	ball	bus
	cheese	shoes		train
	bread	socks		jet
		jeans		
How Many?	5	6	3	5

Questions (color the ○ to show the answer):

Which list has:	Eat	Wear	Play	Ride
1. the most words	○	●	○	○
2. the least words	○	○	●	○
3. the same amount	●	○	○	●

Page 76

© Frank Schaffer Publications, Inc.

Answer Key

Name ______________________________

Directions: Fill in the _____ with north, south, east or west.

- ☑ The kangaroo is north of the monkeys.
- ☑ Snakes are west of the birds.
- ☑ Tigers are south of the seals.
- ☑ The parking lot is north of the gorilla.
- ☑ Seals are east of the gorilla and kangaroo.
- ☑ Lions are north of the bears.
- ☑ Make two cars and one bus in the parking lot.

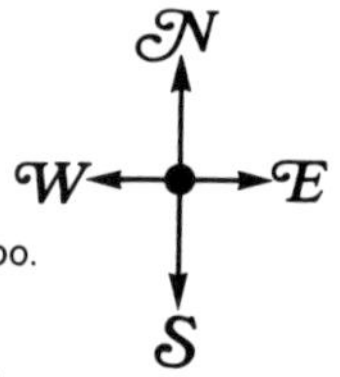

Page 77

Name ______________________________

Directions: In each row mark the problem with the correct answer.

1	5 + 4 = 8 ○	9 − 2 = 7 ●	9 − 7 = 3 ○
2	7 − 5 = 3 ○	4 + 2 = 7 ○	7 − 7 = 0 ●
3	10 + 0 = 10 ●	8 − 6 = 3 ○	5 + 4 = 8 ○
4	6 + 5 = 12 ○	5 + 3 = 8 ●	9 + 2 = 10 ○
5	2 + 6 = 9 ○	11 − 5 = 7 ○	12 − 7 = 5 ●
6	5 + 4 = 9 ●	7 + 2 = 5 ○	9 − 7 = 3 ○
7	12 − 6 = 5 ○	6 + 7 = 9 ○	6 − 0 = 6 ●
8	8 − 7 = 2 ○	8 − 8 = 0 ●	6 + 4 = 8 ○
9	5 − 4 = 9 ○	4 − 2 = 2 ●	9 − 5 = 3 ○
10	12 − 3 = 9 ●	9 + 2 = 12 ○	7 + 4 = 10 ○
11	8 + 0 = 0 ○	9 − 5 = 3 ○	8 − 8 = 0 ●

Page 78

Name ______________________________

Directions: Mark the ○ to show the correct answer.

Sound	Picture	Answer	Sound	Picture	Answer
middle		s ○ n ○ u ●	beginning		g ○ d ● t ○
ending		t ● d ○ c ○	middle		p ○ u ● a ○
beginning		h ● t ○ d ○	ending		g ● l ○ p ○
ending		ch ○ sh ● th ○	beginning		c ● n ○ t ○
middle		i ● a ○ u ○	middle		a ● e ○ f ○
ending		h ○ n ○ d ●	ending		m ○ n ● a ○
beginning	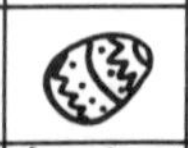	i ○ e ● g ○	beginning		n ● e ○ m ○
middle		a ○ o ● e ○	middle		e ○ i ● w ○
beginning		s ○ z ● d ○	beginning		sp ● sh ○ st ○
ending		k ● g ○ o ○	middle		i ○ w ○ e ●

Page 79

Name ______________________________

Directions:

- ☑ Draw a line under the number one less than 54.
- ☑ Draw a line under the number one greater than ten.
- ☑ Draw a line under the number one greater than 92.
- ☑ Draw a line under the number one less than 80.
- ☑ Draw a line under the number one less than 48.
- ☑ Draw a line under the number one greater than two.

☑ Put an **X** on the numbers you use to count by twos.

1 ~~2~~ <u>3</u> ~~4~~ 5 ~~6~~ 7 ~~8~~ 9 ~~10~~ <u>11</u> ~~12~~
13 ~~14~~ 15 ~~16~~ 17 ~~18~~ 19 ~~20~~ 21 ~~22~~ 23 ~~24~~
25 ~~26~~ 27 ~~28~~ 29 ~~30~~ 31 ~~32~~ 33 ~~34~~ 35 ~~36~~
37 ~~38~~ 39 ~~40~~ 41 ~~42~~ 43 ~~44~~ 45 ~~46~~ <u>47</u> ~~48~~
49 ~~50~~ 51 ~~52~~ <u>53</u> ~~54~~ 55 ~~56~~ 57 ~~58~~ 59 ~~60~~
61 ~~62~~ 63 ~~64~~ 65 ~~66~~ 67 ~~68~~ 69 ~~70~~ 71 ~~72~~
73 ~~74~~ 75 ~~76~~ 77 ~~78~~ <u>79</u> ~~80~~ 81 ~~82~~ 83 ~~84~~
85 ~~86~~ 87 ~~88~~ 89 ~~90~~ 91 ~~92~~ <u>93</u> ~~94~~ 95 ~~96~~
97 ~~98~~ 99 ~~100~~

Page 80

© Frank Schaffer Publications, Inc.

Answer Key

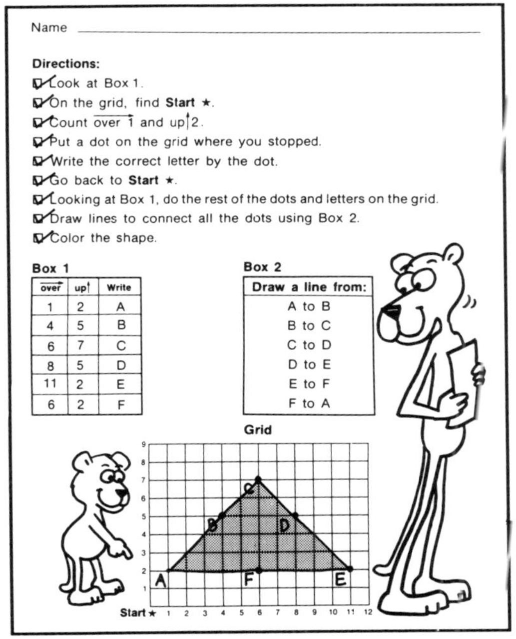

Name ______________________

Directions:

- ☑ Look at Box 1.
- ☑ On the grid, find **Start** ★.
- ☑ Count over 1 and up 2.
- ☑ Put a dot on the grid where you stopped.
- ☑ Write the correct letter by the dot.
- ☑ Go back to **Start** ★.
- ☑ Looking at Box 1, do the rest of the dots and letters on the grid.
- ☑ Draw lines to connect all the dots using Box 2.
- ☑ Color the shape.

Box 1

over	up	Write
1	2	A
4	5	B
6	7	C
8	5	D
11	2	E
6	2	F

Box 2

Draw a line from:
A to B
B to C
C to D
D to E
E to F
F to A

Grid

Page 81

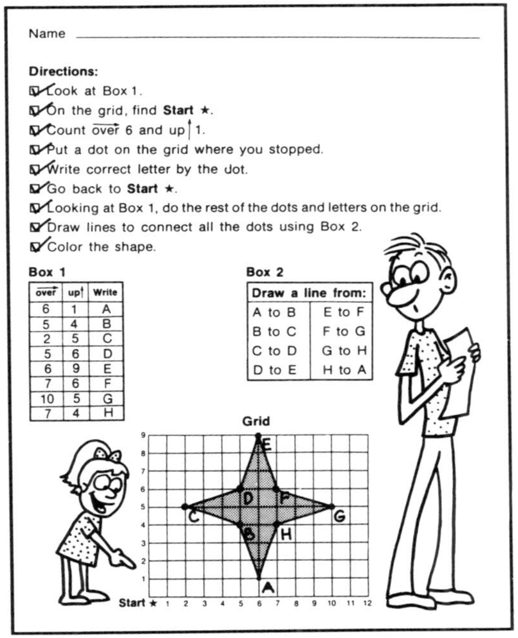

Name ______________________

Directions:

- ☑ Look at Box 1.
- ☑ On the grid, find **Start** ★.
- ☑ Count over 6 and up 1.
- ☑ Put a dot on the grid where you stopped.
- ☑ Write correct letter by the dot.
- ☑ Go back to **Start** ★.
- ☑ Looking at Box 1, do the rest of the dots and letters on the grid.
- ☑ Draw lines to connect all the dots using Box 2.
- ☑ Color the shape.

Box 1

over	up	Write
6	1	A
5	4	B
2	5	C
5	6	D
6	9	E
7	6	F
10	5	G
7	4	H

Box 2

Draw a line from:	
A to B	E to F
B to C	F to G
C to D	G to H
D to E	H to A

Grid

Page 82

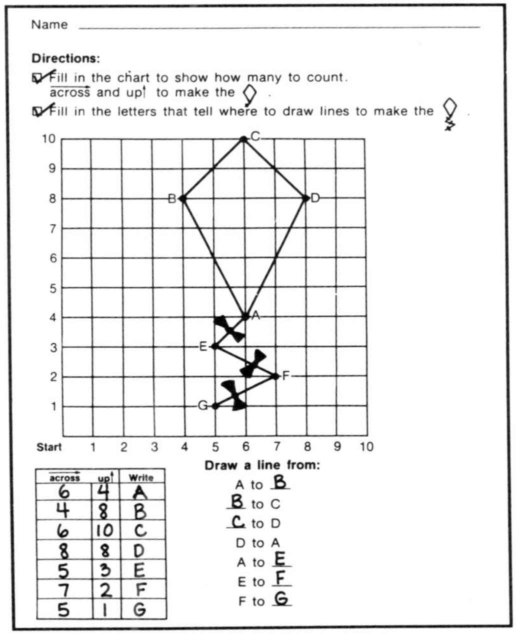

Name ______________________

Directions:

- ☑ Fill in the chart to show how many to count across and up to make the ◊.
- ☑ Fill in the letters that tell where to draw lines to make the ◊.

across	up	Write
6	4	A
4	8	B
6	10	C
8	8	D
5	3	E
7	2	F
5	1	G

Draw a line from:

A to B
B to C
C to D
D to A
A to E
E to F
F to G

Page 83

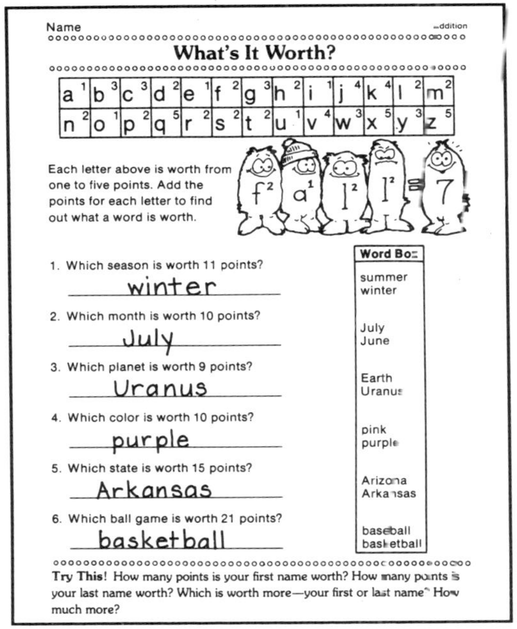

Name ______________________ addition

What's It Worth?

a 1	b 3	c 3	d 2	e 1	f 2	g 3	h 2	i 1	j 4	k 1	l 2	m 2
n 2	o 1	p 2	q 5	r 2	s 2	t 2	u 1	v 4	w 3	x 5	y 3	z 5

Each letter above is worth from one to five points. Add the points for each letter to find out what a word is worth.

$f^2\ a^1\ l^2\ l^2 = 7$

1. Which season is worth 11 points? winter
2. Which month is worth 10 points? July
3. Which planet is worth 9 points? Uranus
4. Which color is worth 10 points? purple
5. Which state is worth 15 points? Arkansas
6. Which ball game is worth 21 points? basketball

Word Box

summer
winter

July
June

Earth
Uranus

pink
purple

Arizona
Arkansas

baseball
basketball

Try This! How many points is your first name worth? How many points is your last name worth? Which is worth more—your first or last name? How much more?

Page 84

Name ______________________

Read the stories very carefully. Think about the **main idea** of each one. Circle the **best** answer.

1. My dad is a fireman. He helps to put out fires in buildings and houses. Sometimes he works all night long. He is very brave.
   a. How to be brave (b.) My dad's job c. A big tall building
2. Think of the things you can find in a book. There are words and pictures, people and places. If you want to know something, look it up in a book.
   a. Thinking about people
   b. Learning new words
   (c.) What to find in a book
3. I live in a yellow and white house. A fence goes all around it. There is a birdhouse hanging in the big green tree. There are many flowers in the garden.
   a. A bird taking a bath b. Going for a walk (c.) A story about my house
4. We have a dog named Moose. Moose likes to eat. Sometimes he eats three lunches and four dinners. Now he is so big he can't fit into his house. Only his head will fit through the door. My dad says we will have to build a barn for Moose to live in.
   a. A late night dinner
   b. Houses that are small
   (c.) The dog who eats too much

Thinking Time

Read the next 2 questions carefully. Then answer them on the back of this paper.

5. Name a job that you would like to have. Describe the job.
6. The fourth story tells about a dog that ate too much. Sometimes people eat too much. Why do you think we might eat more food than we need to?

Page 85

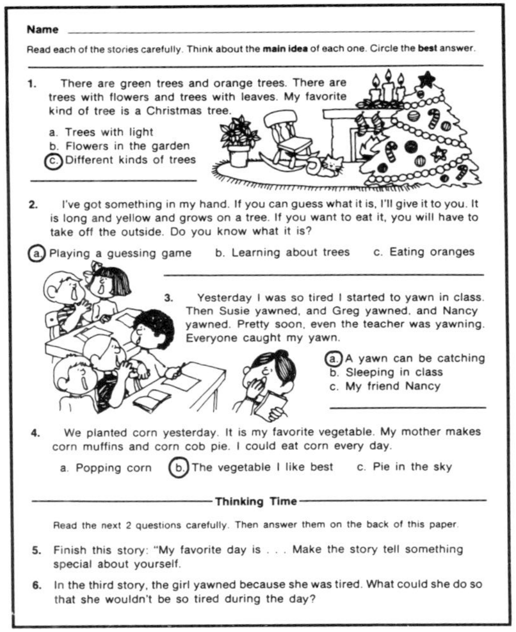

Name ______________________

Read each of the stories carefully. Think about the **main idea** of each one. Circle the **best** answer.

1. There are green trees and orange trees. There are trees with flowers and trees with leaves. My favorite kind of tree is a Christmas tree.
   a. Trees with light
   b. Flowers in the garden
   (c.) Different kinds of trees
2. I've got something in my hand. If you can guess what it is, I'll give it to you. It is long and yellow and grows on a tree. If you want to eat it, you will have to take off the outside. Do you know what it is?
   (a.) Playing a guessing game b. Learning about trees c. Eating oranges
3. Yesterday I was so tired I started to yawn in class. Then Susie yawned, and Greg yawned, and Nancy yawned. Pretty soon, even the teacher was yawning. Everyone caught my yawn.
   (a.) A yawn can be catching
   b. Sleeping in class
   c. My friend Nancy
4. We planted corn yesterday. It is my favorite vegetable. My mother makes corn muffins and corn cob pie. I could eat corn every day.
   a. Popping corn (b.) The vegetable I like best c. Pie in the sky

Thinking Time

Read the next 2 questions carefully. Then answer them on the back of this paper.

5. Finish this story: "My favorite day is . . . Make the story tell something special about yourself.
6. In the third story, the girl yawned because she was tired. What could she do so that she wouldn't be so tired during the day?

Page 86

© Frank Schaffer Publications, Inc.

Answer Key

Page 87

Name ______

Read the stories carefully. Think about the **main idea** of each one. Circle the **best** answer.

1. Look at this camel. Something is missing. Can you find what it is? Fill in the missing part with your pencil.

a. Painting pretty pictures
b. What camels carry
(c) Finding something missing

2. A little dog is called a puppy. A tiny cat is called a kitten and a baby horse is a colt. Does anyone know what a little elephant is called?

(a) Names for baby animals b. Feeding the kitten c. Gray elephants

3. People live in all different kinds of houses. They live in grass houses or ice houses or boat houses. I live in an apartment house. It goes up very high. I can see everyone's house from the top of my house.

a. How to build a house
b. Flying planes
(c) Many different houses

4. I'm going to write a letter to my friend Tony. We moved away to a new city last summer. I will tell Tony all about our new house. I'll ask him to come and visit sometime.

a. Making the letter **B** (b) Writing to a friend c. Paper kites

Thinking Time

Read the next 2 questions carefully. Then answer them on the back of this paper.

5. Moving to a new city can be fun, but it can be sad, too. What things would you miss the most if you had to move?

6. "My house is built on wheels. We can go on a trip to the mountains and take our house along with us." Draw a picture showing what you think this house looks like.

Page 87

Page 88

Name ______

Read the stories very carefully. Think about the **main idea** of each one. Circle the **best** answer.

1. I have a big brother named Danny. I have a mother and father, too. Yesterday, my new baby sister came to live with us. Her name is Bonnie.

a. Big sisters b. Little things (c) My family

2. Bees "buzz", cows "moo", pigs "oink", and birds "chirp". You don't always need to see an animal to tell what it is. Just close your eyes and listen very carefully.

(a) Listening to animal sounds
b. A bird's nest
c. What eyes can see

3. What are hands for? Hands can wave "hello", turn pages in a book and pull a wagon. Hands can pet a kitten, let you stand upside down, and clap when you are happy. What would we do without hands?

a. Waving "hello" (b) All the things hands can do c. Where books come from

4. I lost my first tooth today. His name is Bert. Bert and I have been together for seven years. Tonight I'll put Bert under my pillow and the fairy will take him away. I wonder if Bert will be someone else's tooth tomorrow?

a. Staying up late
(b) What happens to a lost tooth
c. The good fairy

Thinking Time

Read the next 2 questions carefully. Then answer them on the back of this paper.

5. In the second story "close" your eyes means to "shut" them. If you say the "s" softly, "close" can mean something else. What is it?

6. "Everything has gone wrong today. I spilled my juice, lost my book, and shut the door on my finger. I'll be glad when today is over." What is the main idea of this story?

Page 88

Page 89

Name ______

Read the stories very carefully. Think about the **main idea** of each one. Circle the **best** answer.

1. Today is Tuesday. This is the best day of the week. My mother puts three chocolate chip cookies in my lunch—not just two. I wish every day were Tuesday.

a. Eating cookies and milk (b) The best day of the week c. Why I like to eat

2. How many things do you know that are red? There is a sign that says "stop" and a valentine that says "I love you." There is an apple high in a tree and ice cream with a big cherry on top. And then there is me. I have hair that is as red as fire.

a. Stopping at a stop sign
(b) Thinking about red things
c. Where to find snails

3. If I could have three wishes this is what they would be: (1) I would like a 15-speed bicycle that could fly. (2) I would wish for it to be summer all year long. (3) I would wish for three more wishes.

a. A bicycle for Christmas (b) Wishes and more wishes c. A long hot summer

4. "Someone ate your pie, Dad, and I know who did it. A big green worm was hiding under the table. He must have been 20 feet long. When you went into the kitchen he stuck out his tongue and swallowed the pie all at once. Then he crawled out the window."

a. Worms in the kitchen
(b) A pie-eating worm
c. A mad Dad

Thinking Time

Read the next 2 questions carefully. Then answer them on the back of this paper.

5. "John opened the closet door. He clapped his hands and smiled from ear to ear. His wish had come true." How did John feel? How can you tell how John feels if you can't hear him talking?

6. Read the fourth story again. Do you think a worm really ate the pie? Why not?

Page 89

Page 90

Name ______

Read the stories very carefully. Think about the **main idea** of each one. Circle the **best** answer.

1. When I grow up, I want to be a clown in the circus. I can go to many different places and stay up late at night. All my friends will come to see me.

a. Going to bed early b. Taking a trip (c) What I want to be

2. If you want your wish to come true, you need to do three things: (1) Tie your feet together. (2) Jump backwards 12 times with your eyes closed. (3) Throw some water over your head. Be sure to do this outside so your mother won't get mad.

(a) How to make wishes
b. Cooling off in summer
c. 12 things to do

3. Think of all the things your nose can do. It can smell a pie baking in the oven or a candle burning on a cake. A nose can hold glasses over your eyes so you can see. A nose can also give you a cold.

a. Blowing your nose b. Smelling apple pie (c) The things a nose can do

4. Today I bought an orange lollipop. I licked it 56 times. There are still 12 more licks before I get to the stick. But I'm saving them for my dog Bemo.

a. A bone for Bemo
(b) The licks on a lollipop
c. An orange stick

Thinking Time

Read the next 2 questions carefully. Then answer them on the back of this paper.

5. The boy in the first story wants to be a clown when he grows up. Would you like to be one too? Tell why or why not.

6. You shouldn't tell anyone what you're wishing for because then it might not come true. But you can draw a funny picture of your wish and let everyone try to guess.

Page 90

Page 91

Name ______

Read the stories very carefully. Think about the **main idea** of each one. Circle the **best** answer.

1. Animals use their tails for many things. Cows shoo away the flies. A fish uses his tail to help him swim. The squirrel's tail is like a parachute when he jumps through the trees.

a. Animals that swim (b) How animals use their tails c. Squirrels

2. Here is your pumpkin for Halloween. You can put him in the window tonight. But first he needs a face. On the back of this paper draw your own pumpkin. What kind of face will you give him?

a. Baking pumpkin pie
b. Dressing up for Halloween
(c) Drawing a pumpkin face

3. Some animals have names to match the sounds they make. A mouse is called "Squeaky," and a duck is called "Quacker." The name I like best is "Hooty." Can you guess who it belongs to?

a. Animals that squeak (b) Names that go with animals c. Milking a cow

4. Steve loves to tell riddles. Yesterday he told a very silly riddle in class, and this is what it was: "What happened when the boy dreamed he ate a five pound marshmallow?" Answer: "His pillow was gone!" Steve's riddles are very funny!

a. The disappearing marshmallow
(b) A boy who likes to tell riddles
c. Eating in bed

Thinking Time

Read the next 2 questions carefully. Then answer them on the back of this paper.

5. Your eyes can see, your nose can smell, and your mouth can taste. A pumpkin's eyes, nose and mouth cannot do these things. Why?

6. You already know what a tail is, but what does "tale" mean? Use the word in a sentence.

Page 91

Page 92

Name ______

Read the stories very carefully. Think about the **main idea** of each one. Circle the **best** answer.

1. How much wool does a lamb grow every year? About seven pounds altogether. That's enough to make two warm coats or four pairs of pants.

a. Making warm coats b. A seven pound lamb (c) The wool from a lamb

2. DON'T eat with your fingers. DON'T drop your clothes on the floor. DON'T hit your sister. DON'T forget to take a bath. DON'T touch the pie. Does anyone have a DO that I can do?

a. Finding something to eat
(b) Too many DON'T's
c. DON'T forget my party

3. In our town we have a very special store. Only children can go in. The store is so little that big people can't fit through the door. There are toys, games and books inside. It's so much fun. I'll be very sad when I grow up and have to stay outside.

a. Going to a circus (b) A child's special store c. Feeling sad inside

4. "Uh-oh Billy, your mother is coming! She is going to be very mad if she finds a giraffe in your room. This is what we'll do. The giraffe can sit on the bed and then we can put the tent over his head. We'll tell your mom that we're going to camp in here tonight."

a. A camping trip
b. Helping mother
(c) Hiding a giraffe

Thinking Time

Read the next 2 questions carefully. Then answer them on the back of this paper.

5. Finish this story: "I DON'T like to get up in the morning because . . . "

6. Hundreds of people live on an island. There isn't much land left. What kinds of buildings and houses would you build so more people could live on the island?

Page 92

© Frank Schaffer Publications, Inc.

Answer Key

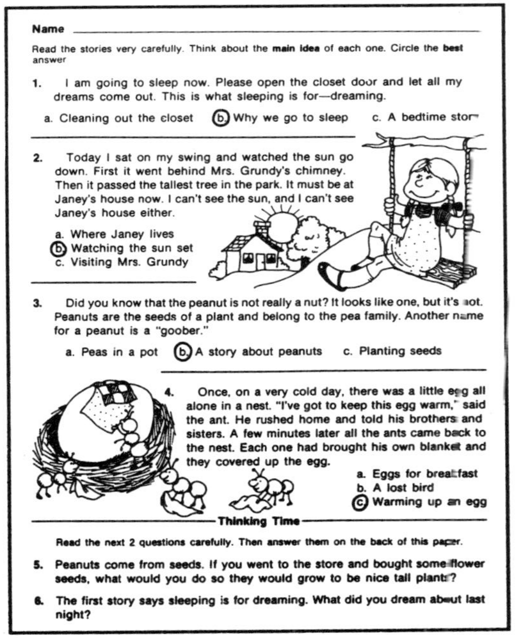
Name ______

Read the stories very carefully. Think about the **main idea** of each one. Circle the **best** answer

1. I am going to sleep now. Please open the closet door and let all my dreams come out. This is what sleeping is for—dreaming.

a. Cleaning out the closet **(b.) Why we go to sleep** c. A bedtime story

2. Today I sat on my swing and watched the sun go down. First it went behind Mrs. Grundy's chimney. Then it passed the tallest tree in the park. It must be at Janey's house now. I can't see the sun, and I can't see Janey's house either.

a. Where Janey lives
(b.) Watching the sun set
c. Visiting Mrs. Grundy

3. Did you know that the peanut is not really a nut? It looks like one, but it's not. Peanuts are the seeds of a plant and belong to the pea family. Another name for a peanut is a "goober."

a. Peas in a pot **(b.) A story about peanuts** c. Planting seeds

4. Once, on a very cold day, there was a little egg all alone in a nest. "I've got to keep this egg warm," said the ant. He rushed home and told his brothers and sisters. A few minutes later all the ants came back to the nest. Each one had brought his own blanket and they covered up the egg.

a. Eggs for breakfast
b. A lost bird
(c.) Warming up an egg

Thinking Time

Read the next 2 questions carefully. Then answer them on the back of this paper.

5. **Peanuts come from seeds. If you went to the store and bought some flower seeds, what would you do so they would grow to be nice tall plants?**

6. **The first story says sleeping is for dreaming. What did you dream about last night?**

Page 93

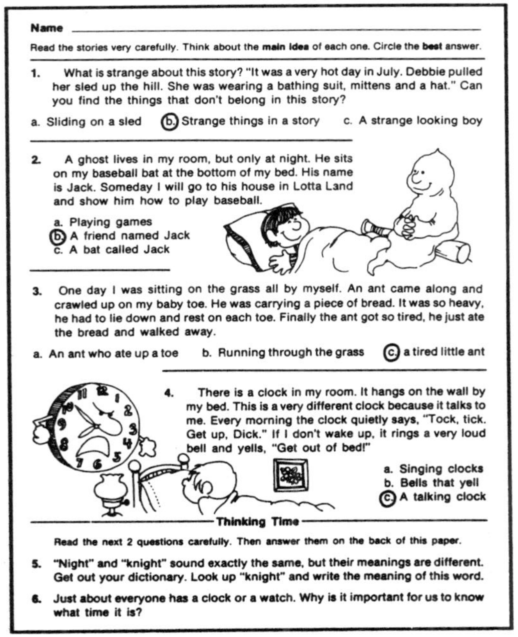
Name ______

Read the stories very carefully. Think about the **main idea** of each one. Circle the **best** answer.

1. What is strange about this story? "It was a very hot day in July. Debbie pulled her sled up the hill. She was wearing a bathing suit, mittens and a hat." Can you find the things that don't belong in this story?

a. Sliding on a sled **(b.) Strange things in a story** c. A strange looking boy

2. A ghost lives in my room, but only at night. He sits on my baseball bat at the bottom of my bed. His name is Jack. Someday I will go to his house in Lotta Land and show him how to play baseball.

a. Playing games
(b.) A friend named Jack
c. A bat called Jack

3. One day I was sitting on the grass all by myself. An ant came along and crawled up on my baby toe. He was carrying a piece of bread. It was so heavy, he had to lie down and rest on each toe. Finally the ant got so tired, he just ate the bread and walked away.

a. An ant who ate up a toe b. Running through the grass **(c.) a tired little ant**

4. There is a clock in my room. It hangs on the wall by my bed. This is a very different clock because it talks to me. Every morning the clock quietly says, "Tock, tick. Get up, Dick." If I don't wake up, it rings a very loud bell and yells, "Get out of bed!"

a. Singing clocks
b. Bells that yell
(c.) A talking clock

Thinking Time

Read the next 2 questions carefully. Then answer them on the back of this paper.

5. **"Night" and "knight" sound exactly the same, but their meanings are different. Get out your dictionary. Look up "knight" and write the meaning of this word.**

6. **Just about everyone has a clock or a watch. Why is it important for us to know what time it is?**

Page 94

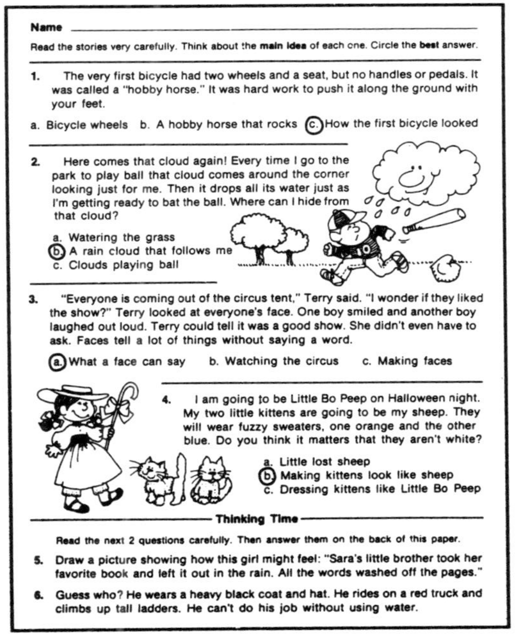
Name ______

Read the stories very carefully. Think about the **main idea** of each one. Circle the **best** answer.

1. The very first bicycle had two wheels and a seat, but no handles or pedals. It was called a "hobby horse." It was hard work to push it along the ground with your feet.

a. Bicycle wheels b. A hobby horse that rocks **(c.) How the first bicycle looked**

2. Here comes that cloud again! Every time I go to the park to play ball that cloud comes around the corner looking just for me. Then it drops all its water just as I'm getting ready to bat the ball. Where can I hide from that cloud?

a. Watering the grass
(b.) A rain cloud that follows me
c. Clouds playing ball

3. "Everyone is coming out of the circus tent," Terry said. "I wonder if they liked the show?" Terry looked at everyone's face. One boy smiled and another boy laughed out loud. Terry could tell it was a good show. She didn't even have to ask. Faces tell a lot of things without saying a word.

(a.) What a face can say b. Watching the circus c. Making faces

4. I am going to be Little Bo Peep on Halloween night. My two little kittens are going to be my sheep. They will wear fuzzy sweaters, one orange and the other blue. Do you think it matters that they aren't white?

a. Little lost sheep
(b.) Making kittens look like sheep
c. Dressing kittens like Little Bo Peep

Thinking Time

Read the next 2 questions carefully. Then answer them on the back of this paper.

5. **Draw a picture showing how this girl might feel: "Sara's little brother took her favorite book and left it out in the rain. All the words washed off the pages."**

6. **Guess who? He wears a heavy black coat and hat. He rides on a red truck and climbs up tall ladders. He can't do his job without using water.**

Page 95

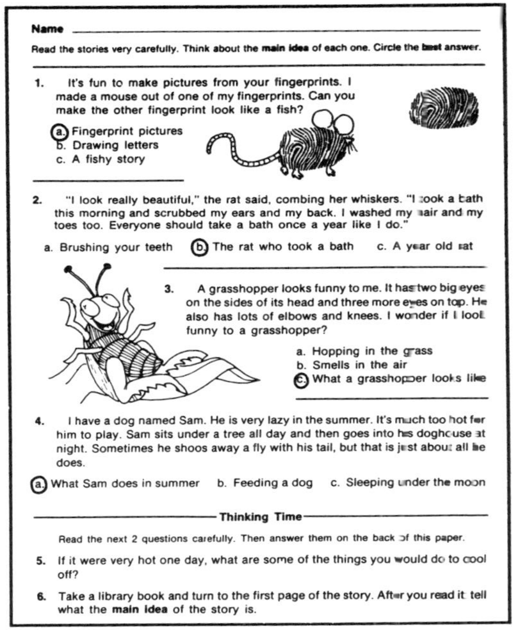
Name ______

Read the stories very carefully. Think about the **main idea** of each one. Circle the **best answer.**

1. It's fun to make pictures from your fingerprints. I made a mouse out of one of my fingerprints. Can you make the other fingerprint look like a fish?

(a.) Fingerprint pictures
b. Drawing letters
c. A fishy story

2. "I look really beautiful," the rat said, combing her whiskers. "I took a bath this morning and scrubbed my ears and my back. I washed my hair and my toes too. Everyone should take a bath once a year like I do."

a. Brushing your teeth **(b.) The rat who took a bath** c. A year old rat

3. A grasshopper looks funny to me. It has two big eyes on the sides of its head and three more eyes on top. He also has lots of elbows and knees. I wonder if I look funny to a grasshopper?

a. Hopping in the grass
b. Smells in the air
(c.) What a grasshopper looks like

4. I have a dog named Sam. He is very lazy in the summer. It's much too hot for him to play. Sam sits under a tree all day and then goes into his doghouse at night. Sometimes he shoos away a fly with his tail, but that is just about all he does.

(a.) What Sam does in summer b. Feeding a dog c. Sleeping under the moon

Thinking Time

Read the next 2 questions carefully. Then answer them on the back of this paper.

5. If it were very hot one day, what are some of the things you would do to cool off?

6. Take a library book and turn to the first page of the story. After you read it tell what the **main idea** of the story is.

Page 96

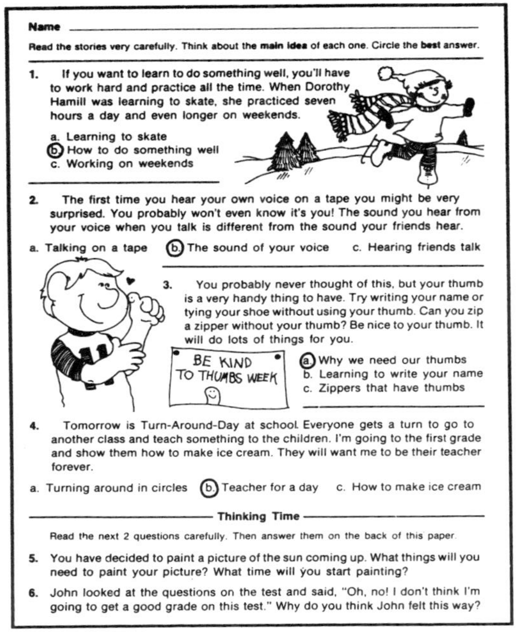
Name ______

Read the stories very carefully. Think about the **main idea** of each one. Circle the **best** answer.

1. If you want to learn to do something well, you'll have to work hard and practice all the time. When Dorothy Hamill was learning to skate, she practiced seven hours a day and even longer on weekends.

a. Learning to skate
(b.) How to do something well
c. Working on weekends

2. The first time you hear your own voice on a tape you might be very surprised. You probably won't even know it's you! The sound you hear from your voice when you talk is different from the sound your friends hear.

a. Talking on a tape **(b.) The sound of your voice** c. Hearing friends talk

3. You probably never thought of this, but your thumb is a very handy thing to have. Try writing your name or tying your shoe without using your thumb. Can you zip a zipper without your thumb? Be nice to your thumb. It will do lots of things for you.

(a.) Why we need our thumbs
b. Learning to write your name
c. Zippers that have thumbs

4. Tomorrow is Turn-Around-Day at school. Everyone gets a turn to go to another class and teach something to the children. I'm going to the first grade and show them how to make ice cream. They will want me to be their teacher forever.

a. Turning around in circles **(b.) Teacher for a day** c. How to make ice cream

Thinking Time

Read the next 2 questions carefully. Then answer them on the back of this paper.

5. You have decided to paint a picture of the sun coming up. What things will you need to paint your picture? What time will you start painting?

6. John looked at the questions on the test and said, "Oh, no! I don't think I'm going to get a good grade on this test." Why do you think John felt this way?

Page 97

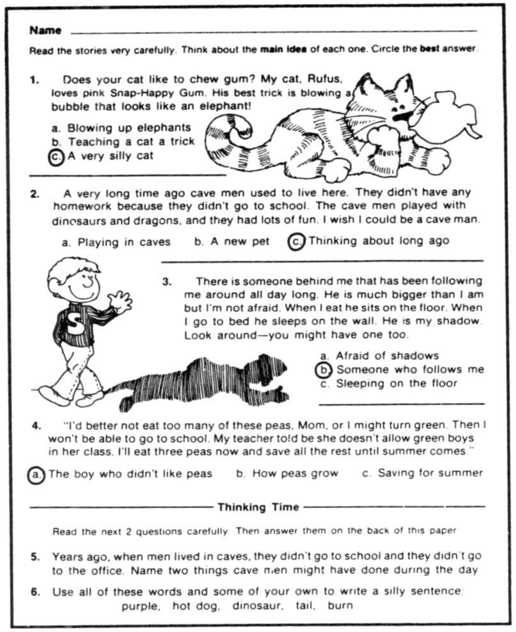
Name ______

Read the stories very carefully. Think about the **main idea** of each one. Circle the **best** answer.

1. Does your cat like to chew gum? My cat, Rufus, loves pink Snap-Happy Gum. His best trick is blowing a bubble that looks like an elephant!

a. Blowing up elephants
b. Teaching a cat a trick
(c.) A very silly cat

2. A very long time ago cave men used to live here. They didn't have any homework because they didn't go to school. The cave men played with dinosaurs and dragons, and they had lots of fun. I wish I could be a cave man.

a. Playing in caves b. A new pet **(c.) Thinking about long ago**

3. There is someone behind me that has been following me around all day long. He is much bigger than I am but I'm not afraid. When I eat he sits on the floor. When I go to bed he sleeps on the wall. He is my shadow. Look around—you might have one too.

a. Afraid of shadows
(b.) Someone who follows me
c. Sleeping on the floor

4. "I'd better not eat too many of these peas, Mom, or I might turn green. Then I won't be able to go to school. My teacher told be she doesn't allow green boys in her class. I'll eat three peas now and save all the rest until summer comes."

(a.) The boy who didn't like peas b. How peas grow c. Saving for summer

Thinking Time

Read the next 2 questions carefully. Then answer them on the back of this paper.

5. Years ago, when men lived in caves, they didn't go to school and they didn't go to the office. Name two things cave men might have done during the day.

6. Use all of these words and some of your own to write a silly sentence: purple, hot dog, dinosaur, tail, burn

Page 98

© Frank Schaffer Publications, Inc.

Answer Key

Name ______

Read the stories very carefully. Think about the **main idea** of each one. Circle the **best** answer.

1. How many things can your tongue do? It can taste your food, lick your lips, say all your L's, and tickle the top of your mouth.

a. How a tongue tastes
ⓑ Good things a tongue can do
c. Tasting food

2. "I have a very bad cold, Mom, and I think I'm getting the measles. I'm much too sick to go to school. I'd better stay in bed all day. What did you say, Mom? Today is Saturday? I'm feeling better already!"

ⓐ Getting sick on Saturday b. A cold day c. Closing the schools

3. I have a big brown dog named Thumpy
He eats too much and looks a little Dumpy
One day, the cat scratched him and made him Grumpy
Now his head is very big and Lumpy

a. Making mother mad
ⓑ A Grumpy, Lumpy dog
c. A big brown cat

4. There are some things that always come in pairs. We have two eyes, two ears, two hands and two feet. Do you think if we had two mouths we could talk to two people at the same time?

a. Hands that talk ⓑ Things that come in pairs c. Drawing a face

Thinking Time

Read the next 2 questions carefully. Then answer them on the back of this paper.

5. Ted is going to get a job. He wants to save $30 before Christmas. Why do you think Ted wants to earn the money?

6. "Poor Nancy! This just isn't her day. This morning she burned her toast, lost her shoe and bumped her head." What would be a good title for this story?

Page 99

Name ______

Read the stories very carefully. Think about the **main idea** of each one. Circle the **best** answer.

1. Hello! I'm a root. I belong to this tree right above my head. I have very long arms and legs. My job is to find water to feed this thirsty tree. Without me trees couldn't live.

a. Drinking a glass of water b. How roots grow ⓒ What roots do

2. I have a pet I'll bet you have never seen before. It is a rabbikangacoon. It has the head of a rabbit, the body of a kangaroo, and the tail of a raccoon. There are only four left in the whole world. It sleeps upside down in a tree at night.

ⓐ A strange looking pet
b. Four animals in a tree
c. Animals of the world

3. You bad old table! Did you see what it did to me, Dad? I was just sitting here eating my breakfast when the table grabbed my arm. It made me spill my milk. You better be nice to me, table, or I'll take you back to the store.

a. Eating breakfast ⓑ Talking to a table c. Shopping for milk

4. Mom said she is going to "dress" our Thanksgiving turkey. I wonder what she is going to put on him, a coat and a hat? I guess she just wants him to look real nice when he comes to the table at dinnertime.

a. Putting a dress on a turkey
b. Setting the table
ⓒ "Dressing" a Thanksgiving turkey

Thinking Time

Read the next 2 questions very carefully. Then answer them on the back of this paper.

5. A rabbikangacoon is a silly animal. Can you draw another funny-looking animal or person and give it a name?

6. All trees have roots. Something you have has roots too. What is it? (Ps-s-s-t, it's something on your head.)

Page 100

Name ______

Read the stories very carefully. Think about the **main idea** of each one. Circle the **best** answer.

1. "Fire" rhymes with "tire" and "smile" rhymes with "while." "Cattle" rhymes with "rattle" and "squirrel" rhymes with "twirl." I'll bet you can't think of a word that rhymes with orange, can you?

a. Twirling a squirrel ⓑ Words that rhyme c. A rhyming song

2. The grass is black, the sky is red,
My cat has feathers, her name is Fred.
"Oink" says the cow, "Woof" says the bee,
I make things the way I want them to be.

a. A cat that barks
b. Painting farm animals
ⓒ Doing things my way

3. Every day the sun comes up in the morning and goes down at night. The sun must get very tired of doing the same thing day after day. If I could be the sun just once, I would rise at night and go down in the morning. But then it wouldn't be daytime, would it?

a. The lazy old sun ⓑ What I'd do if I were the sun c. Getting up in the morning

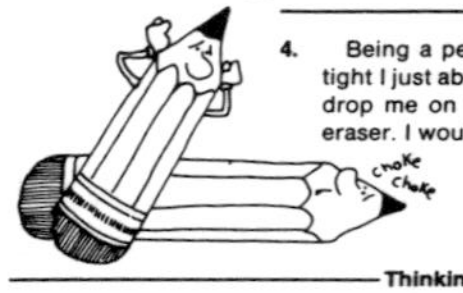

4. Being a pencil isn't much fun. Children hold me so tight I just about choke. They bang me on the table and drop me on the floor. Some children even eat my eraser. I would much rather be a pen living in a pocket.

a. A tight squeeze
b. Eating erasers
ⓒ A pencil who wanted to be a pen

Thinking Time

Read the next 2 questions carefully. Then answer them on the back of this paper.

5. If you could change one thing to look just the way you wanted it to look, what would it be? Describe it in words or with a picture.

6. The first story is about rhyming words. Think of some words to rhyme with these words: bark, candy, lizard, price, skate, straw (Remember, only the endings have to rhyme.)

Page 101

Name ______

Read the stories very carefully. Think about the **main idea** of each one. Circle the **best** answer.

1. Find the ball to go with this sport: There are nine players on the team. The field is grass and shaped like a diamond. It is played in spring and summer.

a. Sports that have balls ⓑ Matching a ball to a sport c. Summer games

2. Did you ever wonder what happened to Jake?
One day he woke up and had turned into a cake.
He only ate sweets and nothing more,
Now he's in a box on a shelf in a store.

ⓐ What happens if you eat sweets
b. Where to buy a cake
c. Waking up a cake

3. I don't like Saturday. I never have. That's the day I have to clean up my room. I don't know why I have to put everything away. The very next day I take it all out again. When I grow up, I'm going to get rid of either closets or Saturdays.

a. How to get rid of Saturday ⓑ The day I don't like c. Growing up in a closet

4. Have you ever seen a doodlebug? He is very little, round and gray. He lives in a hole close to a house. Get down on the ground, whistle near the hole, and call, "Doodlebug! Doodlebug!" He'll come up, but he won't be happy. You woke him up from his nap.

ⓐ A round gray animal
b. Whistling a song
c. Digging holes near houses

Thinking Time

Read the next 2 questions carefully. Then answer them on the back of this paper.

5. The poem in the second story has a funny ending. You finish this poem:
I don't like carrots and I don't like peas
I always forget to cross my t's
But I do like chicken with lots of rice
______

6. What is the one thing you like to do the least? Why?

Page 102

Name ______

Read the stories very carefully. Think about the **main idea** of each one. Circle the **best** answer.

1. Crickets don't make their chirping sounds with their voices. They just rub their wings together. It looks like they are playing the violin.

ⓐ How crickets chirp b. Wings that won't fly c. A violin that chirps

2. The BooHoo is an animal that lives near the sea of VooLoo. He has 16 legs, 3 arms and a tail that looks like a fan. He likes hamburgers best of all. He told me so. Oh yes, the BooHoo can talk too!

ⓐ A very funny animal
b. The sea of VooLoo
c. An animal that eats fans

3. How do you know fall is coming? I can tell because my mom takes my bathing suit and puts it in a box. Outside the air is getting colder and next week I go back to school. These are some of the signs of fall.

ⓐ How to tell when it's fall b. Falling off a bike c. Packing up

4. Do you have some cream of giraffe soup here? My friend eats it all the time. That is how he got to be so tall. I need to get very big by next Thursday. Cowboy Joe is coming to town and he needs someone to rope horses for him. You need to be tall to do that.

a. Riding tall horses
ⓑ Why I need to grow tall
c. Cooking cream of giraffe soup

Thinking Time

Read the next 2 questions carefully. Then answer them on the back of this paper.

5. The word "fan" has two different meanings. One is a thing; the other is a person. Look in your dictionary and write down what each one means.

6. Summer begins on June 21st. Write down some things that remind you of summer.

Page 103

Name ______

Read the stories very carefully. Think about the **main idea** of each one. Circle the **best** answer.

1. Do you know what your name means? "Richard" means "brave" and "Dorothy" means "gift." Every name has its own special meaning.

a. A birthday gift ⓑ The meaning of names c. Names for boys

2. My friend George told me a secret. He said not to tell anyone. I'm the best person to tell a secret to, because the very next day I can't remember the secret. A secret is safe with me.

ⓐ The best secret keeper
b. Remembering late at night
c. Whispering secrets

3. When you sit down in a chair you can make your very own lap. Laps are good things to have. They catch crumbs that fall off the plate. You can put your tired hands to rest in your lap. Best of all, laps can hold a sleeping kitten.

a. Sitting down b. The boy who didn't have a lap ⓒ Good things a lap can do

4. Dreams can take you places you have never been before. You can go by plane, on your bike, or even ride a cloud. Tonight let's go to the City of Ditty. Bring your banjo. The people play music there all night long.

a. Dreaming about planes
b. Moving far away
ⓒ Taking a trip in a dream

Thinking Time

Read the next 2 questions carefully. Then answer them on the back of this paper.

5. "Plane" and "plain" sound the same but mean different things. Write a sentence for each word.

6. Names for holidays have special meanings. What do you think the name "Thanksgiving" means?

Page 104